M000307883

Yin, Yang and You

Note from the Author

In 1981 I assumed the name Mariamne Paulus to express my commitment to take my place publicly as a Light Bearer and as a Wisdom teacher. All books written before the year 2001 carried my given and married names. This series on the Wisdom Teachings, however, is published under the name that carries the frequency of the Wisdom Tradition and that I use in my teaching.

Books by Diane Kennedy Pike

As Mariamne Paulus:
The House of Self
Awakening to Wisdom
Four Paths to Union

As Diane Kennedy Pike:
Life As A Waking Dream
The Love Project Way (with Arleen Lorrance)
My Journey Into Self: Phase One
Life Is Victorious! How to Grow Through Grief
Cosmic Unfoldment
Channeling Love Energy (with Arleen Lorrance)
The Wilderness Revolt (with R. Scott Kennedy)
Search

As Diane Kennedy:
The Other Side (with James A. Pike)

Yin, Yang and You

The Forces of Co-Creation

By Mariamne Paulus

Teleos Imprint ~ Scottsdale, AZ

Teleos Imprint
Wisdom Books
Published by LP Publications
7119 E Shea Blvd
Suite 109 PMB 418
Scottsdale, AZ 85254-6107

Copyright 2010 by Diane Kennedy Pike
All rights reserved.

The Teleos Institute World Wide Web site address is
http://www.teleosinstitute.com

Library of Congress Cataloguing-in-Publication Data

Pike, Diane Kennedy.
  Yin, yang, and you : the forces of co-creation / by
  Mariamne Paulus.
      p. cm.
 ISBN 0-916192-54-7 (alk. paper)
1. Interpersonal relations. 2. Yin-yang. 3. Equilibrium. 4.
Creative ability. I. Title.
  HM1106.P57 2010
  181'.11--dc22

                        2010045358

First Printing, 2010
Printed in the United States of America

Cover Art by Rev. Rebecca Hanna Ph.D., artist and certi-
fied Life As A Waking Dream teacher. For more information
about Rebecca and her work, go to www.wakingdreamwis-
dom.com.

Teleos Imprint
Cascade of Angels

Lily Jean Haddad

DeLorre Haddad

Thomas G. McCarthy

Hollis Johnson

Dorothy Enslen

Vera Isaac

Patricia Elliott

Suzanna Neal

Cathy Young

My Thanks

I am grateful to all those who participated in *Life As A Waking Dream* classes over the years who persistently sought to understand how the Yin and Yang forces functioned in their lives. They helped me to see how important it is to all of us to know how to cooperate with those fundamental energies.

I want to thank Patricia Nerison, Dianne Grasse, and Arleen Lorrance for reading and making suggestions for the improvement of this manuscript, and Rebecca Hanna for her contribution of art to the cover.

Thanks also to the Angels who are named on a previous page for their financial contributions which have made possible the publishing of the *Teleos Imprint Wisdom Book* series.

I dedicate this book to

My Parents
Arlene and Ed Kennedy

[See my Tribute to them in the Postscript.]

The entire cosmos is composed of two natural, complementary forces; yin and yang. Every thought, every action, every impulse and every manifestation is composed of these two. They are opposing, yet one cannot exist without the other. To understand them is a secret of life; to harness their energies is a secret of living.

– Richard Lawrence

When the Solar [Yang] and Lunar [Yin] currents of the Life-Power are rightly perceived, rightly discriminated, and when their operation is kept in proper order, the personality of the [individual] engaged in this practice becomes a free, unobstructed channel for the outpouring of the cosmic life force.

– Paul Case

Contents

The Two Fundamental Energy Polarities

Common Terms Associated with Each

Yin	Yang
Mother Force	Father Force
Feminine	Masculine
Yoni	Lingam
Yum	Yab
Negative	Positive
Magnetic	Electric
Dark	Light
Unconscious	Conscious

Common Symbols of Each

—	✚
__ __	_____
0	. (1)

Symbols of the Union of the Two

Tai Qi Tu

Star of David

Lingum and Yoni

Equal-Armed Cross

Individualized being

Yin and Yang: Mutually Cooperative Energies of Creativity

Have you ever asked, "How did this happen?" or, "How could I be so lucky?" or, "How can I change my life so that I feel more fulfilled?" If so, then you are asking how your life really works, and that is the question this book addresses.

There are two fundamental energies working at every level of your being and of the world. They are the keys to creativity, to harmonious relationships, and to satisfying life experiences. By learning to cooperate skillfully with the dynamic interplay between these two forces, you can become self-reliant, independent, and consciously creative. At the same time you will be able to form deep and productive relationships in all areas of your life.

Even if you do not think of yourself as creative, you are constantly bringing into being your thoughts, your feelings, your actions, your relationships, and your life. You may not think of creative expression in those terms, but I hope by the end of this book you will, because you and only you can create your reality more consciously.

I like to refer to these fundamental energy polarities as *yin* and *yang*. The more common terminology in our Western culture is Feminine and Masculine. However, because those terms are so closely linked to gender identity, I prefer to use gender neutral terms that come to us from Daoism, a Chinese philosophy that dates back to 600 B.C. One of the principles of Daoism is that everything in the universe is an expression of a universal life-force which has two aspects, the yin and the yang, and that is the understanding I want to present to you. If you have few prior associations with the terms I use, and therefore no emotional reactions to them, it will be easier for you to grasp how they function.

The symbol for the yin and yang at the top of page xvii, called the *Tai Qi Tu*, has become very familiar in Western culture. This diagram illustrates that the two forces are actually one whole (represented by the circumference of the circle). The light circle in the dark, or yin, side and the dark circle in the light, or yang, side suggest that neither is totally yin nor totally yang. In addition, the two halves are nestled into one another to illustrate that the two energies are entirely interactive. When yin increases, yang decreases, and vice versa. Neither can function without the other. They are in a totally cooperative relationship as part of one creative force that I like to call the "two-in-one." They are inseparable, complementary, and co-existing energies.

In this book you will learn how to work consciously with the yin and yang energies so that you can be more creative and more effective in your everyday life.

Wisdom Teachings tell us that in the very beginning, two fundamental formative forces united in order to bring into being a third force that would make things manifest. These formative forces might be called Mother-God (Great Yin) and Father-God (Great Yang). The "Child" of this union had within it the attributes of both primal forces, and out of that Two-in-One emerged the process known as cosmos or the universe.

The Divine Triad of Father-Mother-Child appears in all the great religions, though by differing names. What is important to know is that these two fundamental and formative forces are everywhere in creation, from the microscopic level of atoms and molecules to individual human beings to corporations, nations, and even astrological cycles. Once you learn the characteristics of the two forces, you can identify them everywhere around you.

They are also active within you, working in your body, your feelings, your mental processes, and in your spirit. You are a "child" of these two formative forces, and when you learn how to work consciously with the yin and yang you become an agent of co-creation in your own life and in the world around you.

Understanding Yin and Yang

As we begin this exploration of the two fundamental forces, it is helpful to know how to characterize them. Because these creative energies are at work in everything that exists, we use descriptive words that suggest how they function when they are uniting to bring something new into being.* For example, when the yang force initiates, the yin force receives and responds. We are very familiar with that interaction in our human relationships; someone reaches out (yang) and someone responds (yin).

Another example: The yang force guides, directs, and encourages and the yin force nurtures, supports, and acknowledges. An ideal cooperative relationship between school and home would have the teachers guiding, directing and encouraging (yang) the child, and the parents at home nurturing, supporting, and acknowledging (yin) the work being done.

A third example: When the yang force bestows patterns, as when the sperm unites with the egg, the yin force lends substance to give those patterns form. The mother literally shares her bodily substance in the womb while the child is taking form. Also, a strong leader (yang) will outline a powerful business plan, but it is the entire office team that will bring that business plan to life (yin).

Neither polarity is ever devoid of the other. Consequently, when we describe the way each of them functions, we must remember that these are tendencies, not fixed states. If yang energy becomes overly assertive, for example, yin will begin to resist rather than cooperate. We have all experienced that. We are willing to receive guidance, but not if we are dominated or bullied. Then the yang within the yin pushes back, refusing to receive or accommodate; that is, yin becomes more yang. This in turn will usually cause the yang to pull back and become more receptive or less aggressive. In effect, the yang goes more yin.

Or, if yin becomes too receptive, to the point of being almost nonresponsive, having no opinions, making no choices, taking no action, yang may stop giving and pull away. By pulling away and holding back, yang becomes more yin. If yin wants to stay in the relationship it reaches out, expresses appreciation, and invites more in. By reaching out in this way it goes more yang,

These two forces are also inseparable. They always work together. When we speak of them, we identify the function that each performs in relation to the other. For example, yang plants seeds of a new beginning, but unless they are received, held, and nurtured by yin, nothing will come forth from the seeds. Imagine seeds dropped on concrete (which is very hard, yang); they cannot be taken in. But seeds planted in moist soil are held and nourished (yin) until they begin to grow and become a plant or a tree.

Yin, on the other hand, has unlimited resources for bringing forth new life expressions, but if yang never energizes it, yin will produce nothing. I remember a young, healthy apricot tree in our garden that never bore fruit. Our Portuguese neighbor said, "It needs to be grafted." The year after he made the graft, the tree bore fruit. Yin energy could not produce fruit alone; it needed a yang stimulus.

The same dynamic is at work within you. Whereas both the yin and yang forces are powerful, if there is no cooperation between the two polarities within us, you are powerless to produce anything because creative force is released only when yin and yang come together in a dynamic union. You may have many good ideas (yang), but if you never do anything with them to bring them into form (yin), they are not worth much to you or anyone else. As you look at various aspects of your life to learn how to facilitate this union, you will expand your understanding of the functions of the two polarities.

Human beings as a species are divided into two genders, female and male, as are most other animals and many plants. The two genders make reproduction possible. If a male and female come together in just the right way at the propitious moment, a new being eventuates.

This reproductive fact reveals a key to the life process: it takes two polarities to bring a third something into being. In the Hermetic tradition this was called the law of generation. As Manly Hall expressed it, "Everywhere in nature . . . the reproduction of any kind of form, emotion, or thought must arise from the union of two polar opposites." This is the secret of the power to create. By understanding it, we are able to become conscious co-creators with the Cosmic Creative Force, the Two-in-One.

In Appendix One at the back of the book you will find an extensive list of contrasting and comparative characteristics of yin and yang. You may want to make a copy of the list so that you can keep it beside you as you read and as you observe yourself and life in the days ahead.

Part One

Yin and Yang

In Relation to the Outer

2 *Yin, Yang and You*

1

Yin and Yang In Relationships

It is a large undertaking to learn to identify and work with yin and yang energies, but you do not live in a vacuum, and relationships provide you with ongoing challenges and opportunities to develop mastery of these fundamental forces. To be skillful in your daily life you need to learn to express yin and yang energies consciously in relation to others.

By definition, relationship is the connection between two or more people. You have relationships with friends, with family, with colleagues at work, with neighbors, with acquaintances, and with strangers. These relationships are expressed in the way you behave toward others, in the way you feel about others, in what you do, and in the way you express yourself verbally. All these expressions are evidence of the yin and yang forces at work.

Circumstantial Relationships

There are people with whom you relate because your circumstances bring you together. You might meet at the supermarket or in a shopping mall. You might get on an elevator at the same time. Perhaps you live on the same street or go to the same church. Whatever brings you together, the quality of your relating will be determined by how you express yin and yang energies.

Let's look at a customer and clerk in a department store as an example. If the customer addresses the clerk with yang energy, stating exactly what she is looking for by way of a jacket, the clerk will automatically go yin, taking in the information and seeking to facilitate the search. If the clerk locates something she thinks might be right, she will go yang, directing the customer to the rack, taking the jacket off, showing it to her and describing its attributes. As the customer looks and listens, she is in yin, absorbing the data. The clerk may suggest, in yang, that the customer try the jacket on. The customer may agree (yin) and do so.

Such an interaction represents a harmonious interplay of yin and yang in a relationship between two strangers. Suppose however that the customer enters the department in yin energy. She isn't sure what she wants or even if she wants anything. The clerk approaches her in yang energy, saying "May I help you?" If the customer doesn't want to be helped, she replies, "No thank you. I'm just looking." But the yang clerk is not deterred. She persists with questions and suggestions, telling the customer what would look good on her, what is on sale, etc. She probes with questions. The end result may be that the customer will go yang by walking away.

Had the clerk gone yin after the customer said she was just looking, however, it is possible that the customer would respond by going yang and asking questions about where things are located. A back and forth of yin and yang might result.

I'm sure you can recount many occasions when you have left a store annoyed because the salespersons were too insistent (too much yang) or couldn't be found at all (too yin). As the customer, you may not have realized that you helped to create the dynamic. Ignorance of yin and yang complicates relationships unnecessarily. When you experience a salesperson as too assertive, chances are that you withdraw, pulling within (going yin). This only calls forth more yang from the salesperson. On the other hand, if you would meet the yang with yang decisiveness and clarity, knowing what you want and stating it clearly, the salesperson would be likely to go yin, becoming accommodating and helpful.

On the other hand, if you enter a place of business and salespersons are nowhere to be found (yin hiddenness and mystery), a yang "Hello?" or "I need help!" is likely to bring a response, because they do want your business. If you are thinking of the yin/yang dynamic, you can call out for help without waiting until you are frustrated or angry, realizing that a yang thrust is likely to bring forth a response from the yin.

I frequent a store in which I find a wonderful interchange of yin and yang. I go there for office supplies. As I enter the store, I am almost always approached by a sales representative who asks, "Do you need some help?" If I answer "no," he leaves me alone. If I say, "Yes, thank you," he doesn't just tell me where to find what I am looking for, he takes me there and makes sure I find it. If I want to look through things once I get there, I say, "Thank you very much" and he goes away. If I don't indicate that I want to look on my own, he always asks, "Is there anything else I can help you with?" It is a lovely, easy flow of yin and yang that makes shopping effortless. That's the beauty of a harmonious interplay between yin and yang.

To play your part in this kind of relationship, you need to know your function. If you are the customer, be prepared to make your needs or desires known (yang). If you are the sales person, be prepared to offer help (yang) or to step back (yin) if your help is not wanted. Once I went to buy an automobile. I knew exactly what I wanted and told the salesperson (I was yang), who was immediately responsive and helpful (yin). I drove the car and decided to buy it.

At that point, the manager came to "close the deal" (very yang). He began to tell me what a good deal I could get if my credit was good. I told him I planned to pay cash (responding with yang). He insisted that he needed to check my credit so he could give me good "terms" (more yang). I was very firm in saying I planned to pay cash (holding my own in yang). Yang met yang. He would not give up on his determination to get me to buy on credit. I did not give up on my decision to pay cash. So I got up and walked out (yang action). He followed me all the way to the door, saying, "I'll take $1,000.00 off," and then "$2,000.00," etc. (more yang). But by then he had yanged himself and his salesman out of a sale. It pays to know when to go yin. I went to his competitor and bought the car I wanted for cash.

I have heard salespersons complain about customers who are entirely too yin. You go in and say you want to buy, let's say, a printer. The salesperson begins to show you printers (yang), asking appropriate questions to determine what kind of printer would best meet your needs (yin). You are unsure of your needs, you don't know what you like, you can't decide how much you are willing to pay, etc. You are entirely too yin and you consume entirely too much of the salesperson's time before leaving with the statement, "I need to think about it." In yin, you could go on thinking about it for a very long time, to the frustration of all who try to help you.

Similar interactions can occur in job interviews. If you are looking for a job, it is important for you to know what kind of job you want, how much money you need to earn, and what you are willing to do as part of your job. This yang discrimination clarifies your yin desire for work. Researching job openings is also yang. You will want to know as much as you can about the job before applying for it. Writing and submitting your resume is a yang task. Your experience and qualifications should be tailored to the job for which you are applying. When you have completed all these yang tasks, you will go yin by waiting for a response to your application and requesting an interview.

At the interview itself, you should be prepared with questions you want to ask in yin energy as well as statements you are prepared to make about why you want the job in yang energy. After introductions, you will wait in neutral energy to discover whether the interviewer will initiate or invite you to do so. Then you will go with the back and forth flow of yin and yang as the two of you investigate to discover whether you are a good fit for the position.

You should always remember that you are an equal partner. You are deciding (yang) whether to take the job at the same time as the interviewer is deciding (yang) whether he/she wants to recommend that you be hired. Either one of you can say yes, and either one can say no. It is an equal partnership of creative exploration.

Friendships

You become friends with those individuals with whom you have a strong attraction of some kind. It can be physical, emotional, mental or spiritual. You are attracted to them because of chemistry, shared interests, shared values, or shared commitments. Whatever the origin of the attraction, you end up relating to them on all levels: body, psyche and spirit. And no matter what provides the foundation, the course the friendship takes will depend largely on the interaction of yin and yang as you relate. Knowing how the forces work will help you to make conscious choices as the relationship unfolds.

Suppose, for example, that you meet someone while working as a volunteer at a soup kitchen where you are serving meals to the homeless. This volunteer work provides you with both an interest and a commitment in common with the person you meet. However, if there is no attraction on other levels you are not likely to become friends. If you feel an attraction, on the other hand, you may want to get to know the person better. Enter yin and yang.

You can initiate a closer relationship from either the yin or the yang polarity. From the yin polarity, you might say, "Would you like to get a cup of coffee together when we finish today?" This opens a door and if the attraction is mutual, the other will, metaphorically, walk in. The question is yin because you are waiting for a clue from the other before you make your own interest explicit (yang). You haven't said, "I would like to get a cup of coffee with you." You have asked instead, "Would you like to get a cup of coffee?" If the person doesn't drink coffee, he or she might say no to the invitation without meaning to reject you.

Some people do not like to be asked a yin question. They would rather have a disclosure (yang) of your interest or intention. If you were to initiate from the yang polarity, you might say, "I would like to get to know you better. I suggest we go out for a cup of coffee when we finish here." You will notice that this yang invitation makes you more vulnerable, which is the way with yang initiation. You are "out there" with your interest exposed. Even though you go yin to wait for a response, you have already stated your interest and if it is not shared, you may feel rejected.

This little illustration reveals the nature of the difference between a yin opening of an interaction and a yang introduction. In the yin question, the person asking remains hidden and somewhat protected. If the other says "no thanks" it is less of a rejection because you really didn't indicate if you only wanted company while drinking your cup of coffee or if you had a deeper interest in the person. In the yang invitation, the person's interest is exposed. More is at risk.

It is helpful to remember this in human interactions, because we can be more sensitive to others and more responsive, even if we are saying no. Instead of responding "no thanks" to the yang proposal, you might respond "That's a lovely invitation. I am enjoying sharing our work here at the soup kitchen, but I think I would rather get to know you better here before going out together." That's yin energy being discriminating but not rejecting.

If you are responding to the yin question, you may want to get more information before answering. In yang energy, you might say, "Are others going out, too?" or "That would be fun. Shall we invite Marcia to join us?" or, if you are drawn to this person, "Sure. I would like to get to know you better." The first two responses accept the invitation without taking it too personally. The third exposes your interest even though the other has not made a mutual declaration. Now you are vulnerable, but not totally, since the invitation came from the other.

This is definitely Relationship 101, but in the knowledge of how to function consciously with the yin and yang forces, that's where you begin. You want to put the right foot forward, which means you want to establish a back and forth yin and yang flow. Such a flow provides the foundation for a balanced, healthy, and harmonious relationship. If you initiate conversation (yang), be sure to fall silent, wait, and allow (yin) the other to respond. If no answer is forthcoming, ask a yin question: "What about you?" Then wait and listen (yin).

The key to a good relationship is this back and forth flow. If one person does most of the talking (yang) and the other most of the listening (yin), the flow is out of balance. As the one who listens a lot, you will begin to feel as if you have nothing of value to contribute. That may not be true, but the dynamic makes you feel that way. In fact if someone close to you indicates low self-esteem, one of the things you can do is to encourage him to talk to you about his interests and life experiences. When you listen attentively (yin), he will begin to feel he is of value. He is, after all, worth listening to.

If you are verbally and mentally yang by habit, you will need to learn to go yin if you want to form a solid relationship. By inviting the other's opinions and observations and receiving them, you communicate that she is important to you and that what she has to say has value.

On the other hand, if you are verbally and mentally yin by habit, you will need to seize opportunities to open up and reveal (yang) some things about yourself if you are to become acquainted with this person. If you remain silent in spite of probing on her part, she will begin to lose interest and you will have missed on opportunity to launch a new relationship. Shyness is only an excuse, not a reason. If you value relationship, you need to be a full partner in it.

As you build a friendship, there will be a process of discovery. By asking in a probing fashion (yang) and by listening and appreciating what is shared (yin), you will learn what more you have in common. Be sure to observe to see if one of you makes most of the suggestions as to what activities to do together, where to go, what to eat, etc. Though in the beginning of a relationship, the initiating will feel more natural to one of you than to the other, eventually resentment will build up. Even without conscious awareness that this is going on, the initiator will begin to feel totally responsible for the relationship. The question then arises as to whether the other shares enthusiasm for the friendship. The responder may begin to wonder if there is room in this relationship for his or her interests and preferences.

It is not that there needs to be an absolutely equal balance of initiation and response; it is that there needs to be a mutual exchange of energy. It is equally important not to do too much giving in the friendship. If you are always paying for meals, buying theater tickets, giving presents and sending cards, your friend can begin to feel overwhelmed. Even if it is your nature to be generous, too much yang will make the friend feel the need to close up a bit (go more yin) to stop the flow. And you may wonder what caused the withdrawal.

When you observe that you have treated your friend several times in a row, try waiting to allow (yin) the friend to step forward. We all need to feel that we have something to bring to a relationship, and you facilitate that by being willing to receive (yin). On the other hand, if your friend likes you to pay for everything (yang), you may feel taken advantage of, used (manipulative yin).

If you have called or e-mailed or texted (all yang thrusts) two or three times, sit back and wait (yin) for a response. Not everyone moves at the same pace, and if you want to develop a healthy relationship, you will allow your friend to disclose (yang) his or her preferred pace of interaction.

On the other hand, if your friend has proposed activities several times or called or texted you often, you will want to make an effort to come forward out of your natural yin energy and make a yang thrust or two or three. Let your friend know that you value him or her by reaching out rather than always waiting to be invited or pursued.

Romantic Relationships

Friendships can develop into romance if there is a strong chemistry between the two. This is when it is especially important to observe and respect differences in timing. People who are more yang in their personalities move faster and more decisively. If they are attracted to someone, they act with enthusiasm. If the other is more yin in personality, this forward thrust may feel threatening and overwhelming. The one in yin energy moves more deliberately, more slowly, and takes much longer to discover feelings and responses.

As the yang person in a relationship, you need to exercise restraint when you notice the yin partner pulling in or back. Slow down. Back off. Wait. Go more yin. As the yin person, you can help the other by giving verbal clues as to your process. You might say, "I love how enthusiastic and giving you are, and you always seem to know what you want and like. However, I need some time to process (yin) all of this. I like you but I need time to myself to discover what I really want and need."

If you are the yang person, you will definitely want to honor this request. You may want to ask, "Shall I call you in a week or shall I wait for you to call?"

It is not easy to make these choices. You are more comfortable just doing what is natural for you to do. However, if you want to build a relationship then you will be wise to apply what you understand about the yin and yang.

If you are not sure about your friend's pace in relating, you can ask, "Am I moving forward too quickly for you?" or, "Am I too quick to make suggestions regarding our next date or activity?" Or, on the yin side of the dynamic, "Do I seem to be dragging my feet in this relationship?" or "Am I too slow to respond when you ask me something?" It is unusual to ask such a question because most people are completely unaware that differences in timing and pace affect a relationship. The other may need time to reflect before answering the question, but in the long run, you will be glad you asked.

You can pick up clues about differences in yin and yang preferences or habitual relating. If you say, "I'd like

to meet your parents," and you feel the other withdrawing, you can immediately respond with, "Does it feel too
soon to you?" Instead of asking such a question, most
people feel the closing of the yin energy and assume
that it means the other doesn't really like you or never
wants you to meet the parents, instead of just indicating
a difference in pace.

Supposing you say to your lover, "Do you want to
get married?" and you immediately feel withdrawal.
Recognize that your yang thrust was too sudden or too
direct. Instead of calling the whole relationship into
question, reframe the question: "I mean, do you eventually want to marry someone?" This immediately takes
the pressure off and leaves room for a genuine response.
If the answer is yes, you can either pursue in yang energy,
saying "I keep fantasizing about marrying you," or you
can stay in yin and wait for an indication as to whether
you are a candidate.

If in your eagerness you say, "Do you want children?" and the other responds with a look of shock,
you can follow up with, "I don't mean that you and I
will immediately have children together. I was asking
a more general question." Even if your question was a
reflection of your own readiness to have children with
this person, you can widen the area of interest (a yin
expansion), giving the other room to breathe.

The yin and yang flow is not just on the verbal and
emotional level. Physical actions also express yin and
yang forces. Suppose every time you go out, your date
waits (yin) for you to open the car door (yang) and that
becomes annoying to you. If you recognize the pattern
as expressing yin energy and you would rather see more
yang, you could say, "Why don't you drive tonight?" Giv-

ing up the driver's seat indicates that you are willing to go yin. If your date refuses, you can have a discussion about the importance of sharing.

If your date always picks up the check before you have a chance when you go out to dinner, you can say, "I would feel more comfortable if I shared in paying for our dinners." If your date is not comfortable with that, again you have an opportunity to explore whether you are equal partners in this relationship.

Some people continue to act out of old societal paradigms in which men were expected to carry the yang responsibilities and women were expected to always go yin. Although this is less frequent these days, studies have shown that often once a couple is married the old paradigm kicks in on unconscious levels. You will want to watch for indications of this. If you begin to feel resentment that you are always in the yin position, or always expected to be yang, talk about it. This is a new age and equal partnership is the new paradigm. Roles are defined more by preference, interest and ability than by gender or societal expectations.

Sexual Engaging

In any relationship, instincts will carry you without any thought or feeling into a full expression of sexual intercourse if you do not make a different conscious decision. We are "wired" to procreate, so the body responds in ways that fulfill this mandate to preserve the species even if the specific sexual intercourse is not going to result in a pregnancy.

Most people who engage sexually are not intending to procreate. They are just doing what comes naturally.

Someone initiates (yang). Someone responds (yin). And before very long, sexual intercourse is the result. Chemistry has ruled the day. The strong attraction between two has led to an instinctive physical expression.

However, as exciting and pleasurable as such intercourse is, it is not necessarily the best foundation for a relationship. If you are interested in a long-term relationship, you need to start observing the yin/yang dynamics in your sexual exchanges. Do you always initiate (yang)? Do you wait for the other to respond (yin), or do you just plunge ahead? Do you ask what pleases your partner (yin)? Do you tell the other what pleases you (yang)? Do you disclose (yang) your feelings after the love-making? Do you wait (yin) for your partner to share about the love-making, or do you bound out of bed and get on with tasks that await you (yang)?

If you are too yang, you will probably touch, embrace, or kiss without asking the other or assessing readiness and willingness. You may talk too much about yourself and not invite your partner to share with you. You might assume you know how your partner feels without asking, and thus offend without intending to do so. Be sure to invite your partner to participate equally.

If you tend to be too yin, you will probably go along with what your yang partner suggests whether or not it is what you want because you will be eager to please. You may hesitate to say no even when you want to. And you may expect your yang partner to know what you want and need. You need to speak up for yourself, expressing what pleases you and what doesn't and asking for what you need and want.

Some people are reluctant to talk about their love-making, as if to put words on their feelings will somehow destroy the "magic" of the instinctual chemistry. However, the opposite is really the case. Chemistry alone will only carry most couples through two years of relating at the most. If the psyche is not brought in to join the fun, the instinctual fires will die out and both partners will lose interest in sexual engaging.

Feelings are an essential part of love-making. If a vital connection is not made on the feeling level each time you engage sexually, the exchange will not be harmonious. And thoughts are more important than most people imagine. Both men and women have been influenced by impressions, beliefs, values, and past experiences. If you never bring these thoughts out into the open they will interfere with sexual engaging in the long run.

Instinctual chemistry that leads to sexual engaging is exciting and rewarding. The strength of it sweeps us up and carries us to a climax. If the relationship is to last, however, conscious monitoring of the yin and yang of love-making is essential.

Many jokes are made about who ends up "on top." This is an unconscious awareness that when we are "on top," we feel dominant (yang). If you always insist on being on top, you devalue your partner's participation. There are also many jokes about men initiating and women saying, "Not tonight, dear. I have a headache." This is a recognition that the initiation is often left up to the yang partner who is made to feel like a nuisance.

If you are in a long-term relationship, you will want to make sure that there is a balance of yin and yang between you. By initiating, you indicate to your partner that expressing your love sexually is important to you. If your partner initiates, be responsive (yin). This indicates that you, too, want to express your love sexually.

Be experimental (yang). Try new ways of expressing your love (yang). Be willing (yin) to try the new things your partner proposes. If you don't like them after trying them you can say so.

In the midst of your love-making, express what you especially like (yang): "That feels so good! I really like that. I would prefer that you fondle my breasts rather than going down on me. Would you take me in your mouth? Etc." When your partner expresses a preference, respond to it (yin) in order to please your partner and to discover how you feel about it.

After the climax, take time together to share what was good and what you would prefer. Be honest and also kind. Don't take your partner's preferences as criticism. Instead, be grateful for what you learn that will help you to better express your love. If you run into subconscious resistance, talk about it (yang) instead of burying it (yin).

If you want to have an exciting and fulfilling sexual life in your long-term relationship, this kind of verbal communication is essential. It will lead to deep trust and intimacy. Without it, either you will both lose interest or one of you will impose your preferences on the other and both of you will build resentment. Of course it is possible to be too analytical (too much yang) instead of simply reporting what you are feeling and what you experience. And sometimes an expansive yin appreciation for the beauty of what is will be enough to nurture the love between you.

The important thing is to be partners who express in both yin and yang.

Love and Intimacy

We all long to love and be loved. One way to define love is that it is the strong bond between yin and yang, both within self and between self and another. Love is experienced in the body as a strong attraction to another, and it awakens a longing for shared space ("I want to be with you."), shared activities ("I enjoy doing things with you."), and shared physical contact ("I can't keep my hands off of you!"). Love is also experienced as a feeling. It begins with "I like you" and then develops into "I want you." Love is recognition of mutually shared values and beliefs and of intellectual pursuits. "I love the way you think." Or "I love how your mind works." Love is also an opening of the heart to unconditional love. "I love you for who you are, not for what you say or do." "I love you just the way you are." And love can also be a spiritual attraction. "I feel I have always known you." Or, "Perhaps you are my soul mate."

In any of these examples, the defining characteristic is a feeling of strong attraction followed by the forming of a bond. When it is love, the bond is strong and often unbreakable.

However, not all love leads to an experience of intimacy. Intimacy requires trust, and that trust is built by a consistent back and forth flow of yin and yang energies on all levels.

Two who are strongly attracted physically need to discover what each likes and what makes each feels nurtured and fulfilled. Otherwise, two bodies meet but no bond forms. Only in the interchange of yang initiations and yin responses do two come to know each other well enough to trust that the physical relationship will be satisfying for both. It doesn't happen automatically. It takes conscious attention to the other and willing acceptance of responsibility for self in the relationship. In other words, if your needs are not met it may be because your partner is not paying attention, or it may be that you are not expressing what you like and want.

On the emotional level, trust is equally important. When deep feelings are shared (yang) it is essential that the partner receive and acknowledge (yin) those feelings. The best indication that a feeling has been received is if you verbally expresses what you heard. If your partner says, "I was deeply hurt by what you did yesterday," you can respond, "You felt hurt by what I did." At first you may find such a response awkward, but if you want emotional intimacy, it is essential. This is sometimes called "active listening." You not only listen, you verbally indicate what you heard.

There are several ways people miss the opportunity for emotional intimacy. A common error is to respond to what your partner says with, "I know just what you mean. When I . . ." Your intention is to indicate that you have received your partner's sharing, but what you actually do is to turn the attention from your partner to yourself. It is never true that we know "just" what someone else means. Our past experiences are too different because our inner lives are a blend of all that has gone before in our life. If you respond this way, your partner is almost certain to close up and feel that you have not heard him or her.

Another way we destroy a moment of emotional intimacy is to respond to a sharing of feeling with a denial of the other's feelings. Your partner says, "I am so discouraged I just want to quit." You say, "You don't mean that," or "You don't really feel that way." To indicate your understanding you need instead to acknowledge the feeling. "It's natural, when you are discouraged, to want to quit." This can be followed with, "Do you want to share what makes you feel so discouraged?" Your child says, "I hate you!" Rather than say, "Of course you don't hate me" you could say, "I hear that you hate me right now. Is it because I sent you to your room?" Your lover says, when you approach physically, "I am afraid." Instead of responding, "I'm not going to hurt you," you could ask, "What are you afraid of?" and then go yin to listen and receive the response.

One final way we destroy emotional intimacy is to assume that we know how the other feels without asking. If you say, "I know you don't trust me," or "I know you don't like my friend," or "Why do you hate my mother?" you have made a yang thrust which threatens the other and will more than likely cause a withdrawal into yin rather than an open sharing.

No feeling lasts forever and most last for only a few seconds, so we should not be afraid of any feeling. Once expressed and received, feelings change. But if negative feelings are not acknowledged, they grow stronger, and if positive feelings are not received, they weaken.

If you have a feeling you are afraid to share because you imagine that your partner will respond negatively, begin by saying, "If I share what I am feeling, will you promise to listen until I finish before you respond?" Then be sure to invite your partner's response and be equally respectful, listening all the way to the end.

Responsiveness in emotional interactions is essential to a feeling of closeness and trust.

Intimacy on the level of thoughts, beliefs, and opinions is especially difficult to achieve because we are used to debating ideas rather than exchanging them. Again, it is essential to let the other know that you have heard what was expressed. Often, when exchanging on the mental level, we wait for the other to quit talking so we can express our own ideas and opinions. This is the most nonproductive kind of conversation. If we want intimacy, we need to pay special attention to the back and forth of yin and yang. When your partner expresses a belief, receive it, say what you heard, and then explore with yin questions that draw out more. Only after you have remained in yin for some time should you shift to yang, either in response to an invitation or on your own initiative.

When a bond is formed in heart-centered love and in spirit, mutual respect is essential to the development of spiritual intimacy. Two who acknowledge each other as beings of deep value express that by respecting the other's convictions, intuition and knowing. If your partner says, "I have a strong feeling that I need to develop my talents as an artist," rather than assessing whether this is a practical course to pursue, you will want to express support and encouragement to follow his or her heart. If your partner says, "I need to have a place where I can be alone to do my study and meditation," you will want to begin immediately to explore how the two of you can make that happen. Inner spiritual impulses are never up for discussion. They are very personal and unique to the individual. Intimacy develops when those impulses are totally respected and honored.

Long-Term Relationships

There is a song written by Neil Diamond and Alan and Marilyn Bergman that goes like this:

"You don't bring me flowers, you don't sing me love songs, you hardly talk to me anymore. . . I remember when you couldn't wait to love me . . . Now after lovin' me late at night when it's good for you and you're feeling alright, well you just roll over and you turn out the light, and you don't bring me flowers anymore. It used to be so natural to talk about forever, But 'Used to be's' don't count anymore . . . The romance is gone out of the relationship, settling into habitual ways of relating, and you don't bring me flowers anymore."

This wonderful lyric captures the reality of many long-term relationships. When the romance goes out of the relating, consciousness needs to replace chemistry. Whereas in the flush of romance, chemistry motivates you to express your love in flowers and long conversation, in the long haul, habit takes over and that can be deadly. Habit is unconscious. Habit takes no effort. Habit is boring.

The only cure for habitual relating in long-term relationships is consciousness. When you are conscious, you observe what is going on and you make choices to change things according to what is important to you. All personalities settle into inertia when given the opportunity. That is, we prefer to go along with things the way they are rather than seek to change them. But this inertia is deadening, and if you want your long-term relationship to thrive, not just survive, then you need to make the conscious choice to find ways to express your love and appreciation. If not by bringing flowers, then by going out, or taking a vacation together, or learning to dance, or inviting new friends over, or, or, or.

When the romance is gone, which means chemistry is no longer driving your relating, it is time to very consciously initiate the new. Conscious interaction is life-giving.

Too often, partners in a long-term relationship begin to blame each other for the deadness that has set in instead of consciously infusing the relationship with new life. If you are the one who wakes up to the fact that romance is dead, then you are the one who needs to infuse new life into the relationship by initiating (yang) new activities, new expressions of your love, new interests. Too often couples resort to having another child or remodeling the house when new shared activities are needed instead. Wake up! Take the initiative (yang). Be responsive (yin). Come to life (yin/yang).

2

Yin and Yang In Families

The relationships you have with family members are largely circumstantial, but chemistry also plays a big part. You are thrown into relationship with parents, children, siblings, in-laws, and extended family by what is sometimes called the accident of birth. Whether or not your birth was an accident, you may wonder how you came to be part of this particular family.

Parents

Your predominant relationship is with your parents. In archetypal images, the father is the yang force in the family, establishing and enforcing the rules, being the provider and protector, setting an example for how to be successful in the world, and so forth. The archetypal mother is seen as the yin force, providing unconditional love, acceptance, nurturance, comfort and a warm and safe home to return to.

In fact, however, sometimes father is more yin than mother, and these days both father and mother may hold jobs out of the home and work together to provide the warm and safe home to return to. Or, as is often the case, there may be only one parent in the household or there may be two parents of the same sex. In other words, parents are human beings who differ from the archetypal norm according to their individual preferences, interests, skills, and life circumstances.

Understanding yin and yang can help prevent confusion. Children need models for both archetypal forces. From the unconscious level, children are going to expect the father to model yang energy and the mother to model yin energy. If the parents are conscious of the yin and yang they can help the children to process the ways in which they, as individuals, differ from the archetypes.

Suppose you are the father, but you happen to have a lot of yin energy. As a consequence, you choose to do a lot of the nurturing and caretaking of the children. You are at home a lot, you cook for them, you get them ready for school in the morning, you are there when they return home from school. Your wife, however, works during the day. She is an executive in a large company and she exercises a lot of yang energy. She brings home more money than you do and she is highly motivated to achieve. She often talks to the children about their interests and skills, encouraging them to do well in school so they can make a contribution in the world.

It would be extremely helpful to your children if you could point out to them the nature of the yin and yang energies and tell them that you are an expression of more yin energies than their mother, even though yin is more often associated with women. You could help them to see how your wife manifests yang energy, even though yang is more often associated with men. You could then tell your children that your examples, as their parents, show them how free they are to express these yin and yang energies in ways that are harmonious for them.

If you are a single parent, you will have an opportunity to teach your children about the balance of yin and yang forces in each individual, as we will discuss in Part Two of this book. If you point out how you are expressing each of the forces in your personality and in your relationships with them, it will be easier for them to affirm the balance of their own creative forces.

Same sex parents have a unique opportunity to point out that the physical body does not determine how we express yin and yang forces. Chapters 4 & 5 will help you to see how to present such insight into the creative polarities.

Since archetypes work in our subconscious minds and very few people are aware of this, your consciousness of these two forces enables you to give your children an enormous gift. You can help them to avoid stereotyping about gender roles in society and to feel comfortable with their own predispositions. When you as a parent are comfortable with who you are, your children will be at ease, too. They might otherwise feel there is something wrong with them or with their parents, without knowing why they feel that way.

Also, as your children grow and you begin to observe their behavior and their preferences, you will be able to make them aware of how they are manifesting the yin and the yang.

It is also very important to observe how you relate to each of your children. Because their personalities differ from one another, you will need to adjust your own relating if you want to be in a harmonious relationship with each of them.

If you tend to be yin in your personality, notice which of your children is also predominantly yin and which is predominantly yang. As the yin parent, you will be eager to listen to your children, to support them in their endeavors, to see that they have the resources they need for all their activities, etc. A child who is also yin may not share much with you or express needs and desires. You may have to stretch yourself to be more yang with that child. You will want to reach out with questions and comments. You will want to ask for opinions, preferences, observations, and feelings. You will want to honor the child's need to have privacy while being vigilant to include him or her in family activities. Some parents, in an effort not to intrude, allow the yin child to withdraw and never share. That is not good for the child and it is certainly not helpful to you as a parent.

If you tend to be yang in your personality, notice which of your children is also yang, and which is predominantly yin. As the yang parent, you will tend to give a lot of guidance and instruction to your children. The yin child might quietly acquiesce to whatever you say. The yang child, on the other hand, may push back, resisting your direction and insisting on independence. Although you will feel good about the acquiescent child, you should also recognize that every child needs to develop his or her own preferences. It will be important for you to reach out to the yin child, inviting conversation and making sure to listen and appreciate all that is shared. In relation to the more yang child, you will want to acknowledge ideas and preferences and affirm him or her for venturing forth to follow his or her dreams. Although the yang child may have to follow your rules in your house, you can acknowledge that the day will come when he or she is on his or her own and can make independent decisions about such matters.

Each relationship is different, of course, but a parent who is more yin than yang needs to realize that children need yang energy to set boundaries for them and to hold firm to those boundaries while they develop their own sense of what is right and wrong. Children also need to learn about the consequences of their actions if they disobey rules or cross boundaries. These consequences need to be laid out by a yang force and enforced. The enforcement needn't be harsh and it should always be fair, proportionate to the violation. But discipline in the home helps a child to develop self-discipline, discrimination, and values. If the yin parent needs to defer to the more yang parent for the sake of the children, then so be it. As a single parent, however, you will need to express yang energy even if it is not your most developed polarity.

Likewise, children need to feel loved unconditionally. They need to know they are loved even when they have been "bad," and that they do not have to earn love through their performance at school or their choice of activities and friends. Children also need to feel safe in their home environment and nourished by not only food but attention. A yang parent needs to recognize how essential these things are to the development of the child's self-esteem and self-confidence. If the yang parent is not comfortable being the nurturing parent, he or she should gratefully defer to the yin parent to give the children what they need. And the single parent will need to consciously develop the yin polarity if need be.

Understanding the yin and yang can help parents to monitor what they are able to give to their children and to support each other in providing what is natural and easy without feeling competitive or jealous or as if they are failing when they do not prefer the archetypal yin/yang expressions.

If your child never talks to you, examine the yin/ yang dynamic. Do you initiate too much or not enough? Are you too passive? Are you present enough, sharing common space and activities, to provide opportunities for the child to share? Do you listen? Do you actively express interest in what your child is doing at school and after school? Do you express your love? Do you tell your child when you are proud of him or her? Do you share some of what is going on in your life without burdening your child with your adult concerns? Do you share your values and beliefs, while listening to what is important to your child and what your child believes?

In all these ways you will establish a balanced back and forth of yin and yang expression, helping your child to feel close to you and you to feel close to your child.

Children

We were all children once, and for many of us, the imprints of those early experiences live on and continue to dictate our behavior in many circumstances. If we had understood the yin and yang forces, we might have made our transition into adulthood with greater grace and understanding.

Children are in the yin position in a majority of their interactions. They are yin to their parents, to their teachers, to their older siblings, and to many of their peers. In large part that is because children are in the midst of a steep learning curve. Everything is new to them on all levels. Because they lack experience, they are pretty much dependent on others to tell them and show them how things are done either directly or by example, and they must be in yin energy to receive direction, feedback, and impressions.

The electronic era has introduced new challenges. Children remain mostly yin when they are listening to music on iPods or watching videos and movies. They exercise some yang discrimination when they choose what to watch or listen to. Playing video games they have more opportunities to practice yang skills, but they are functioning within parameters provided by the game-maker. And although texting provides a nice yin/yang flow of sporadic communication, it does not teach young people human interaction skills on a face to face level.

For all these reasons, children may not have sufficient opportunities to develop their yang force of initiation, discrimination, and choice-making. Children are usually not considered old enough to make their own decisions (a yang skill) without adult supervision. Consequently, even fledgling yang forays often get knocked down by criticism or failure, which can lead to a lack of self-confidence and courage.

Parents can evoke a greater balance of the creative forces in their children by encouraging them to make choices and express preferences whenever possible. There is an art to giving guidance without imposing your preferences. Many parents are reluctant to allow their children to choose foods, clothes, friends, and activities because they are afraid the children will not conform to their own images of what is right or good. In fact if children are allowed to choose they are more likely to follow their parents examples than if their parents try to force them to do so.

Most adolescents begin to exercise yang energy.

They may initiate interactions with peers, express their opinions (usually parroting their parents' opinions) and preferences, occasionally stand up for themselves when challenged by peers, and begin to identify their dreams and aspirations for the future. In relation to their parents, they attempt to be less yin by resisting input. This is really a closed yin rather than an expression of yang energy. Often they actively rebel, choosing the opposite of what they know their parents want. This is an expression of yang energy, but it is a reaction rather than a forceful initiation from their own preferences.

If children have been encouraged to make choices as they are growing up, they feel less need to rebel as adolescents. They have developed their own preferences and have a basis for making choices based on those preferences. If parents respect their right to experiment and try out new things, adolescents find it easier to continue to respect their parents.

Siblings

Usually older siblings are yang to younger siblings. They seize the opportunity to exercise "authority," mimicking their parents, because they can. However, not all younger siblings are willing to acknowledge this pseudo authority, and they may resist and protest. If you examine the relationships you had with your siblings while growing up, you will be able to discover how the yin and yang energies were played out between and among you. Sibling interactions, including sibling rivalry, are excellent practice sessions for interactions with peers. As a consequence, those who grew up with siblings often develop relational skills earlier than only children.

However, chances are not good that any children will understand how the yin and yang forces are at work in their relationships unless parents teach them about the creative polarities.

Many of us arrive at young adulthood without having discovered our own preferences, without having developed our own opinions, and without having developed our decision-making skills. Moreover, we often have not developed a strong sense of self that makes it possible for us to enter into peer relationships with those who hold positions of authority. As a consequence, we too often assume the yin position in interactions, waiting for others to initiate, assuming others know better, allowing others to boss us around, and failing to assert and express our own strengths and skills. In effect, we too often assume the yin position of the child when we are chronologically adults.

Some people, on the other hand, over-compensate for their lack of yang development. They become domineering adults who attack rather than initiate, control rather than guide, and overwhelm rather than inspire. Such people often end up in leadership positions, but they are not good yang leaders because they do not have confidence or wisdom in their yang expressions.

To fully develop our potential as individuals, we need to develop a balance of yin and yang both within ourselves and in our interactions with others. Relationships within families can encourage this development, especially if the parents are conscious of the two forces and understand how they work together. Then they can model both energies and teach their children about them.

3

Yin and Yang In Society

During the past two thousand years, our social interactions took the form of the parent (yang) / child (yin) paradigm. This meant that in every social context, each of us quickly assessed (usually unconsciously) our position in society, recognizing that we were either in the parental position of authority (yang) or the child position of obedience (yin).

The "Traditional Family" Archetype

The family provided the underlying archetype for all social relationships. In traditional families, the parents (but principally the fathers) were seen as the authority figures. This meant that father not only knew best but also had the power to enforce his knowing. Father was seen as the head of the family. He had the social and moral authority that entitled him to execute his judgment as he sought fit. He had ultimate power and control. He was, in effect, the reigning yang force.

In this archetype, the mother was essentially invisible, remaining in the background where she supported and carried out the father's will. She was the archetypal yin force, her power hidden and expressed primarily as support for the reigning yang. (A minority of cultures around the globe maintained the matriarchal structure of the previous two thousand years in which the mother was the authority figure, but the parent/child paradigm ruled, nevertheless.)

The children were completely subservient to the father's will in the traditional family. They had no free choice. They were dependent on the father's generosity, and if it was not forthcoming, they did without. They were not able to determine their own fate.

This archetype, which is now referred to as the "traditional family," influenced all societal structures. Governments were seen as parents (yang) whose duty it was to rule over and provide for their children, the citizens (yin). The heads of governments were powerful leaders (even if female) who reigned supreme, whether they were admired and respected or feared and hated. Citizens felt essentially powerless to determine their own fates. They were dependent on the good will of the rulers or representatives, and when that was lacking, they suffered.

Even in the family of nations, large empires (yang) acted as parents to relatively powerless small nations (yin). In the 20th Century in the West, a "cold war" was fought over whether "Mother Russia" or "Uncle Sam" would take over the parental role that had been vacated by the British Empire. In the East, the Japanese Empire had been defeated and China tried to remake itself in the image of the emerging Partnership Paradigm, with mixed results. Peasants were empowered and old rulers deposed, but gradually the revolutionaries reverted to the parental ruling practices of the old regime.

Religions in the West were structured in the image of the same family archetype. In both Judaism and Christianity, God was viewed as "Father"; whether capricious or loving, He was all-powerful (yang). Often religious leaders (priests and ministers) were also called father, and the occasional female leader was usually referred to as mother. Church members were referred to as children, or more offensively, "flocks of sheep" (yin).

School systems were organized in the same way. Teachers and professors were seen as the authority figures (yang) that had all the knowledge. Students were the empty vessels (yin) that came to them to be filled with that knowledge. Teachers and professors had absolute power and control in their classrooms, with authority to punish students who did not obey them. Teachers and professors, however, were subservient (yin) to the administrators who had the power to hire and fire (yang).

In the workplace, it was understood that owners were the ultimate authorities (yang). They held all the power and delegated some of it to supervisors, overseers, or foremen. All workers were viewed as fortunate to be taken in by owners, as if by being hired they became members of a family with no more power over their own fate than children (yin).

Other Reigning Archetypes

There were, of course, exceptions, but the exceptions only helped to prove the rule. All rebellions, revolts, reform movements, and "grand experiments" were made in opposition to the governing paradigm of yang over yin.

Although the "traditional family" archetype reigned supreme, other archetypes were also powerful within the overall paradigm of parent/child. Royal archetypes, for example, retained their power into the 20th century. King and Queen and their children (prince and princess) held sway (yang) in the kingdom. All others were "subjects" (yin) who were looked after by royalty as long as they were loyal and obedient to that higher will.

According to Christianity, God was seen as the King of the Universe (ultimate yang). The Queen of the Universe was deposed and only the "one and only son" could act on the King's behalf. The rest of us, as subjects (yin), were to establish the kingdom here on earth by doing God's will, that is, by obeying the Great Yang.

Other variations of the royal archetype were the strong leader or ruler, the tyrant, and the dictator (overpowering yang). Under the latter two, the subjects became servants and slaves (subservient yin).

Another principle archetype was that of the savior. Since the children were powerless, their only hope for a better life came in the form of the supreme "rescuer." Archetypes that were reflections of, or secondary expressions of, the savior were the hero, the messiah, the rescuer, and even the helper.

In all cases, the children were seen as defenseless victims, powerless to help themselves, dependent on outside intervention, always yin to the ruling yang. Occasionally the martyr archetype would elevate the victim. By sacrificing self, the martyr acquired power to ignite the imagination of the masses, and sometimes the masses would act as one body to overthrow the ruling authority. However, inevitably the new regime would resort to the same parent/child paradigm.

A New Paradigm Emerges

The parent/child paradigm ruled supreme throughout the 20th century, but a new paradigm began to weaken it. The new paradigm is an expression of the interaction between the yin and yang forces that we are exploring in this book. It acknowledges **Partnership** as the most powerful relationship possible.

Partnership challenges the old rules. Instead of absolute power being held by the yang head of the family, power is shared among peers through a balanced yin and yang interaction. Authority is no longer automatically attributed to the few who are in positions of power. Instead, authority is acknowledged as belonging to all adults with respect to their own lives and futures.

Knowledge is no longer held by the few. Instead, information is available to all who have access to technology and have acquired the skills to use it. A new value is given to wisdom as the knowledge of how to integrate learning gained through life experience with moral sensitivity and life skills.

Another big shift is the recognition of personal responsibility. Instead of the masses being children who cannot be held responsible since they have no power or authority, in an age of Partnership every individual is held responsible for her/his own choices. All citizens share responsibility for the commonwealth or the republic.

Chaos Precedes Form

All societal structures are faltering under the influence of this emerging paradigm. The traditional family archetype no longer holds absolute sway. Increasingly, fathers are forming partnerships with mothers and are seeking new ways to parent that will endow their children with self-esteem and the ability to make wise choices regarding their own futures. Same sex parents are learning how to partner in a family context. And single parents are learning to embody a partnership of yin and yang forces within themselves as they raise children able to assume responsibility in new ways.

Governments are wrestling with how to express this new paradigm. The communist vision was of a government in which the people would share wealth and power equally. It was not possible to move so quickly from one paradigm to another, and most communist experiments failed miserably. Nevertheless, the urge to topple hierarchical regimes has permeated nearly all cultures. The only question remaining is how can this new Partnership Paradigm be given expression in governments? Will new technologies make it possible to bring democracy into practical expression? Or does a new governmental form await us?

Religions are struggling to adapt to the pressure of the new paradigm. In some congregations, husband and wife are partnering as ministers and rabbis, and liturgies have been given more egalitarian forms. More women are being given positions of power and authority. But fundamental patterns of church rule continue to conform to the old paradigm in most cases, and as long as religions focus on correct belief, they will need authorities to tell people what to believe.

School systems are staggering, unable to find a way to shift paradigms. The result is near chaos in many schools where authority is no longer automatically acknowledged by new generations of students, and old ways of teaching no longer command respect. Partnering with other teachers and team-teaching have brought the energy of the new paradigm into the schools, but the full expression of it has yet to emerge.

In the workplace, active experimentation with teams who work together has brought some success, and a few companies have moved to shared ownership. However, the transition is stressful for all concerned. True transformation is slow to occur.

New Archetypes Help
To Empower the Paradigm

New archetypes assert their influence gradually and it is not yet clear which ones will be most powerful. For now, it appears that the savior archetype is being replaced by the "co-creator" archetype. In this archetype human beings function as partners with God-the-creator, who is no longer viewed as all-powerful but rather as a partner with humans in the enterprise of creation. Creational theology sees God as interdependent with the creation, and the godhead is viewed as a partnership of "mother-father" or "yin-yang."

The global grief ritualistically expressed at the time of Princess Diana's death may well have been an indication of our intuitive awareness that the royal archetypes are withdrawing into the background. We grieved for what had been central to our understanding of the structure of reality. We now stand in the barrenness of not-knowing with regard to what will take the place of royalty.

In the twentieth century we watched the death of the strong leader and hero archetypes in the cooperative overthrow of Hitler and in the assassination of Gandhi, Martin Luther King Jr., John F. Kennedy, and numerous others around the world. Other strong leaders have died natural deaths, but have not been replaced (Mao Tse-tung, Churchill, FDR, DeGaulle, etc.).

The United States government, structured as a three-way partnership between Legislative, Judicial and Executive branches, has yet to emerge as a practical demonstration of the Partnership Paradigm. The members of the Judicial Branch do not fancy themselves as partners with the other two branches. The legislators refuse to cooperate with each other, each seeking to embody the old paradigm of powerful leader. And the President and his fellow Executive branch helpers look for ways to lead legislators who have no interest in following. And so the chaos grows in Washington. It may need to reach a crisis level before strong wills bend to the new paradigm.

The new archetype of leadership may well be the consensus builder. The Clintons attempted to establish this archetype during their first year in office. Hillary was viewed as too strong and Bill was considered too weak. They were forced to abandon their effort to build a consensus and to return to the old competitive mode. The public seemed not to be ready for a Partnership Executive, sneering at the "two for the price of one" concept. Nonproductive competition has not only continued and grown more hostile, but the electorate has yet to demand a consensus, sticking with the win or lose mentality.

The other phenomenon that has occurred is that moral lapses among politicians have completely abolished the illusion that moral authority belongs to the strong leader. Perhaps the Pope is the only "king" who is still perceived to be wearing clothes, and he is increasingly called into question, even with regard to the enforcement of morals within the clergy. All other strong leaders are now recognized as "mere mortals."

Perhaps this is why the public has been so lenient in its attitude toward moral lapses, not only in politicians but also in sports icons and media stars. It is as if a sigh of relief has gone through the society. Pretenses are at an end. The president, for instance, is now seen as "one of us," no better and no worse. We are not looking to him to set the example for how to conduct our personal lives. We are only asking that he "do his job." We will attend to our own values and ethics, thank you very much.

New Skills and Attitudes

The challenge before us all is to learn the skills and attitudes essential to the new paradigm of partnership. We need the self-esteem that comes from knowing how to work with both yin and yang energies. We will assume responsibility for our own lives as we claim the power that lies within us to create our lives more consciously. We must learn to respect others and to value differences. We must learn consensus building and conflict resolution, which are expressions of the skill of directing the yin and yang forces. We must acknowledge the awesome privilege and responsibility of co-creation. Scientists are leading the way in that arena as they learn not only to clone creatures in their laboratories but to create live cells. We must reawaken our sense of the sacred in all areas of life and come to know ourselves as spiritual beings who express our true nature in ever-expanding diversity.

As the new Partnership Paradigm becomes stronger and the archetypes that give that paradigm expression exert more and more influence we will learn what other attitudes and skills we need in order to bring it into full expression.

We are privileged to be alive during this transition. We can stretch ourselves to align in frequency with the new that is emerging and help give form to new societal structures by developing our individual skills in the expression of yin and yang energies.

Part Two

Yin and Yang

Within Self

46 *Yin, Yang and You*

4

Yin and Yang In Your Body

At the heart of everything that exists, two polarities of energy, the yin (feminine force) and yang (masculine force), function in a powerful union. It is the exchange of force between these two that causes things to come into being. Not only did it take the union of sperm (yang) and egg (yin) to bring your physical body into form, but the two fundamental energy polarities, yin and yang, continue to operate within you, physically, psychologically, and spiritually. Without them you would not be able to think, to speak, to act, to love, to feel, or to live.

Your physical body is formed "in the image" of the two forces. By studying the differences between human females and males on the level of form and function in the reproductive act, you can discover essential qualities that characterize these invisible forces.

The human reproductive organs mirror many of the qualities and functions of the yin and yang, helping us to identify them. If we focus on the generative organs themselves and the way they function, not on roles played by females and males during the act of sexual intercourse, we quickly discern the characteristics of yin and yang. Throughout human history, these reproductive organs have been used as symbols for the yin (the womb or yoni) and the yang (the phallus or lingam) because they reflect universal qualities of the creative forces.

It is essential that these characteristics not be viewed as sex-role stereotyping. Rather, the qualities the sex organs exhibit during sexual intercourse mirror two invisible forces at work everywhere in nature.

The female's reproductive organs, which symbolize the yin polarity, are hidden and undisclosed. From the outside, no one can see her vagina, ovaries or womb. Her readiness to engage in sexual intercourse is made known in subtle clues rather than any observable changes in her physical form. She may seem to soften and become warmer while within herself she may feel a stirring and moistening in her vagina. She is generally slower than the male to become aroused and to release the fluids that ease the way for the penis and the sperm. However, she has tremendous staying power and can often sustain her state of readiness for long periods of time. Her attention tends to be more diffuse and global and she often takes more pleasure in the process than in the outcome. She is not as goal-oriented as is the male.

Her part in the act of union is to be open and receptive. Her movements and her scents may attract the male, drawing him to her. Her magnetic attraction is often evocative even though indirect. Once she takes in the penis, she holds it, rhythmically drawing it further into her depths. Her ovum waits in expectancy, and as the sperm approach, the ovum opens and takes into itself the sperm of her choice. The ovum is responsive to the secret language of the genetic code carried by the sperm. For nine long months her womb provides a container within which a being takes form. She nourishes the fetus by giving of her own substance.

By contrast, the male, who symbolizes the yang polarity, pursues, stimulates, and arouses the female so that she will be prepared to receive him. His penis becomes hard in order to penetrate the vagina of the female. He thrusts the penis into the female and energetically probes and excites her until his own gift of semen is released.

Each of the sperm swimming in that semen is capable of catalyzing the reproductive process, but it takes a prodigious expenditure of energy for the sperm to swim upstream until they find the ovum. They must be quick, vigorous, dynamic, goal-directed, and unrelenting or they will not succeed in their life-giving task, for they are short-lived.

The male's reproductive organs are revealed and exposed. His ability to function is obvious when the penis becomes erect. He is often quickly aroused and quickly spent. He must remain single-focused or he will lose his ability to function.

The reproductive process, made evident in the functioning of the male and female organs, reflects many of the principal qualities and characteristics of the yin and yang polarities. However, this does not tell the whole story, because your body, whether male or female in gender, is actually a balance of the two forces and even the reproductive organs reflect this balance. For example, testicles are the yin supportive energy for the male penis. Each testicle is a container, a holding place, where sperm are birthed and nurtured to maturation. This is a yin function. Likewise, although the female womb is a yin container, it nevertheless manifests yang qualities in its assertive, birth-pushing function which thrusts the child into life.

The sexual organs of the male and female provide easy illustrations of the two polar energies, but accurately identifying how those energies are at work in your body requires a more extensive exploration.

Yin and Yang Qualities in Your Body

Whether you were born female or male, your body is a balance of yin and yang energies. The balance is not always equal. Sometimes a body is more yang, sometimes more yin, but both polarities are always present.

When bodies are predominantly yang, they tend to be taller and leaner than more yin bodies. This is because it is characteristic of the yang force to elongate and of the yin force to expand. To a great extent these qualities may be genetically influenced, but diet and exercise can modify the genetic predisposition. Even though the height of a body cannot be changed, the shape and texture of it can be. There is a section about diet and exercise below. For now, let us continue to look at how the two forces manifest in your body.

When a body is more yang, the muscles tend to be harder and stronger. The more yin energy in a body, the more flexible and adaptable the muscles are, but they may have less strength. Yang energy lends more force and intensity. Yin energy can make muscles more delicate and soft.

We summon yang energy when we want to move fast and work hard. When we are ready to unwind and relax, we call up yin energy. For long, sustained efforts of any kind, a good balance of yin and yang energy is required. Yang energy burns hotter and therefore is more quickly exhausted. Yin energy is cooler and is able to sustain efforts over longer periods of time without becoming depleted.

When making love, we use yang energy to initiate, to invigorate, and to excite. Yin energy makes us approachable, receptive, and responsive. For sexual intercourse to be fully satisfying to both partners, each one needs to express through both polarities.

Assess your own body. Look at it in the mirror, touch it, and sense it from within. Then list the yin qualities and the yang qualities to determine which polarity predominates or whether there is a good balance of the two forces in your physical make-up. If your body is too yin or too yang, you can help to restore balance by diet and exercise using the guidelines below.

Diet

There are some broad principles you can follow regarding yin and yang energies in the food you eat. These guidelines will help you to balance the yin and yang forces in your body by eating with more discrimination.

Generally speaking, food can be divided in the following way: all fruits and vegetables are yin; all meats are yang; grains and cereals are a balance of yin and yang.

The most yin food has the highest sugar content. When you ingest it, your body is bound to expand and form more fatty tissue. Alcoholic beverages and soft drinks are the most yin of any foods. Next on the spectrum would be fruits. Fruit juice is more yin than the fruit itself. The larger (more expanded) fruits are, like melons and grapefruit, the more yin. Smaller fruits are slightly more yang, like grapes, cherries, and apricots. Leafy, expanded vegetables are more yin, like cabbage and lettuce. Smaller leafy vegetables, like Brussels sprouts, are more yang. Vegetables like broccoli and asparagus are more yang than leafy vegetables because they are harder and, in the case of the latter, elongated. Nuts and seeds are less yin (more yang) than most vegetables and fruits. Beans are the least yin (most yang) of vegetables.

Animal foods are yang, except for cheese and milk, which are yin. Fish and poultry are less yang than pork, but pork is less yang than beef and eggs, which are the most yang food.

Stimulants, like coffee, are yang; depressants, like alcohol and most drugs, are yin.

Grains, rice, and cereals are an almost perfect balance of yin and yang.

These designations can help you to understand why a diet based on lean meat will help build strong muscles and a more lean body. A vegetarian diet will build more soft tissue and will tend to add fat to the body.

That said, it should also be noted that the way the food is prepared and cooked alters the balance of yin and yang. When food is cooked, it becomes more yang, and the longer it is cooked, the more yang it becomes. If salt is added, it becomes more yang. Raw foods retain their basic qualities of yin or yang. While eating a full spectrum of vegetables and fruits, including seeds, can yield a good balance of yin and yang, it is usually necessary to add grains and beans to hold the balance if certain vegetables and fruits are out of season and hard to get.

To evaluate food, consider whether it is expanded, soft and/or watery (yin) or contracted, hard and/or dry (yang), whether it has a mild taste and odor (yin) or strong smell and taste (yang), and whether it cooks quickly (yin) or slowly (yang). For example, comparing celery and carrots using these characteristics, we can see that celery is more yin than carrots.

Although meat is more yang than vegetables, in the United States nearly all our animals are raised to be fat, making them far more yin. When we eat the meat (yang), we also take in the fat (yin). When you add that factor together with how much sugar most people take in, through alcohol, soft drinks, sugar-coated cereals, etc., and how many dairy products we eat, it is easy to understand why our population grows more obese (more yin) with each passing year. [For a complete presentation of yin and yang in our diet, read *The Macrobiotic Path to Total Health*, by Michio Kushi and Alex Jack, A Ballantine Book, Random House, 2003.]

Many Eastern philosophies teach that the food we ingest affects our emotions and thought processes. They advocate vegetarian diets, which are yin, as a way of curbing aggression and agitated thinking, which are excessive yang. This raises the question as to whether America is an aggressive culture, prone to violence, due in part to the amount of meat we eat. And do people instinctively eat too much sugar and fat (yin) as a way to bring balance to the meat (yang)?

If you find you do not have enough yang energy to get started on projects, you could ask yourself whether you need to take in more protein to give you more yang fire. And by contrast, if you are constantly fired up and on the go, would it help to eat more vegetables in order to mellow out?

Exercise and Daily Activities

Perhaps you can already identify the difference between yin and yang exercise. Running is a very yang exercise because of the speed and the energy expenditure. Runners tend to be thin and their muscles hard. Walking is more yin; it is slower and not as tiring. Swimming tends to be a balance of yin and yang. Most people who are not swimming competitively feel relaxed as they swim. They use their muscles actively, but do not push themselves. Tai Qi is another balanced form of exercise, whereas other Eastern martial arts tend to be much more yang. Yoga is generally a balance of yin and yang, though there are variations that go from very yin to very yang.

Ballroom dancing is more yin than contra dancing, but both are more yin than break dancing or hip hop dancing. Football and hockey are more yang than basketball and soccer, though all of these sports are more yang than tennis or golf.

In order to decide whether to choose an exercise that is more yin or more yang, observe yourself as you move through your day. If you are seated a lot, at a desk and/or in a car, you will want to choose exercise that gives you maximum movement (yang) to balance your inactivity (yin). You will not want to move from your desk to the car to your couch in front of the television. This would be far too much yin for your body, and you might find that your body is restless at night and not ready to sleep.

On the other hand, if you are constantly on the move during the day (yang), waiting tables, attending customers, building houses, delivering mail, caring for young children, etc., you will want to choose a form of exercise that provides some relaxation and stretching (yin), like Yoga, swimming, or walking.

Climates and Seasons

Your body also responds to climates and seasons, and you need to adapt your diet and exercise to keep balance during those cyclic changes.

Summer is the yang (hot) season and winter is the yin (cold) season. Spring and fall are transitional and tend to be a balance of yin and yang, neither very hot nor very cold. In the summer you will want to eat more fruits and vegetables (yin) to balance the external yang, and during summer (yang), swimming, yoga or Tai Qi (yin) are more appropriate exercises than running or jogging (yang).

In the winter, a yin season, you will automatically gravitate to hot foods (remember that cooking makes everything, even vegetable soup, more yang), and you will probably eat more meat (yang). The colder (more yin) the winter, the more vigorous should be your exercise, even though it is sometimes difficult to motivate yourself to go outside when it is cold. It is interesting to note that the most yang of the group sports are played in the fall and winter, like football, hockey, and basketball, and the more yin sports in the spring and summer, like baseball, swimming, and tennis.

In addition to seasonal changes, there are variations in climate. Some climates have lots of rain and humidity (water is yin). Others are dry (yang). A cold and dry climate is a balance of yin and yang; a hot and dry climate is extremely yang. A cold and wet climate is extremely yin, whereas a hot and wet climate is a balance of yin and yang. Seasonal changes within those climates may alter the balance of yin and yang and you need to be responsive to all those factors as you pay attention to your diet and exercise and the effect of your surroundings on your physical well-being.

Gender

One of the strongest influences on the balance of yin and yang in your body is gender. Those who are born in female bodies tend to display more yin characteristics: softer, rounder, plumper, and often shorter. Those born in male bodies tend to show more yang qualities: leaner, taller, stronger, and harder. However, as we all know, these are only tendencies and generalizations and they are by no means always true. There is a broad spectrum within both genders. Male bodies can be extremely lean or very fat; very tall or short; very strong or weak; very hard or soft, and everything in between. Female bodies also vary greatly from very round to angular; from very fat to skinny; from very short to very tall; from quite weak to extremely strong.

During adolescence, when strong gender identity is developing, boys pay a whole lot of attention to the size of their penises (a pervasive symbol for the yang force), to whether they are able to get an erection (an outward indication of the yang force) when they want one, and to whether they are able to suppress an erection when they don't want one. Adolescent girls notice whether or not they are developing breasts, how big the breasts are, whether or not that is a good thing, and whether their menstrual flow has begun. In later stages of female gender identity, the widening of the hips (expansion is yin) making it easier to carry a child is something to which the female pays attention.

Concerns arise in us about how the body functions and whether it has the right equipment when we are identified with the gender of the body. The word 'gender,' according to Webster's New World Dictionary, is an archaic variation of the word "engender," meaning to beget, to procreate, to generate, to create, to produce, to bring into being, to bring about, to cause. Nature seeks to perpetuate the human species. The instinctive concern about gender, therefore, stems from the urge to procreate, even though that urge may be primarily subconscious in adolescence.

However, although gender influences your body and your thoughts and feelings about it, it does not determine the balance of yin and yang energies.

Sexuality

Sexuality is determined by the chemical charge in the cells of the body, not by gender. Most male bodies carry a predominantly positive/electrical charge (yang) and most female bodies carry a predominantly negative/magnetic charge (yin). However, there is a spectrum in both male and female bodies. Not only does the charge vary from very strong to very weak, but sometimes male bodies carry a negative/magnetic charge and female bodies a positive/electric charge.

Sexual attraction between two persons depends on chemical interactions and there is not much you can do to alter those responses. If you carry a strong electrical charge, you will be attracted to those who carry a magnetic charge. The stronger the opposite charge is, the stronger will be the attraction you feel. If on the other hand you carry a weak charge, either electric or magnetic, you will not feel a strong attraction to another unless they happen to carry a very strong charge, whether opposite to yours or not.

It is for this reason that many people are confused about their gender identity. On the one hand, it is fairly easy to determine whether a body is male or female in gender. However, until now there have been no instruments to determine what chemical charge a body carries. If someone with a female body feels a strong attraction to other females, it may be because her body, though female in gender, carries a positive/electrical charge. And someone in a male body may feel attracted to other males because his body, though male in gender, carries a negative/magnetic charge.

Those whose bodies do not carry a strong charge can sometimes feel an attraction to either gender. This is why a man or woman can marry and bear children, fulfilling reproductive and societal expectations, and be reasonably happy until later in life when they discover that they would really prefer a same-sex relationship. Others, whose chemistry is more clearly defined, would find it repugnant to engage sexually with someone of the same charge because same charges repel each other.

In that regard, our bodies function like magnets. If you put the positive ends of two magnets together, they repel each other, as do two negative ends placed together. But positive and negative together are not only attracted to each other, but they firmly bond to each other. Bodies are the same. They are attracted to the opposite chemical charge and with the opposite they form a tight bond. If they are not strongly attracted, they will not form a strong bond.

In the next chapter we will look into the relational aspects of sexuality and matters of gender identity. On the level of the physical body itself, it is helpful to know that gender does not determine sexuality, and gender identity (whether you feel/know yourself as a male or female) is a different issue from your sexual identity (whether you are attracted to men or women or neither or both).

Understanding that both yin and yang are at work in our bodies makes it possible for us to work with those polarities consciously to achieve the results we desire. Begin now to observe your body so that you can achieve a reasonable balance in yourself on the physical level.

60 *Yin, Yang and You*

5

Yin and Yang In Matters of Identity

Because each of us is born in either a female or male body, issues of identity arise in us early in life. Many people think of themselves as a "girl" or as a "boy" from the time they are very small. As they mature that gender identity grows into knowing self as a "woman" or a "man." Because this is a very common experience, it is perplexing to the majority that there are others who either don't think of themselves as gender-specific or who feel they are the opposite gender from what their body seems to indicate. And to that minority, issues of gender identity often run very deep and cause much suffering.

Let's look into these issues from the perspective of the yin and the yang.

Societies work hard to teach young children appropriate behavior for girls and boys. Even if this teaching is not conscious (yang), it is powerfully expressed by example and implication (yin). For example, if boys are given cars and trucks to play with rather than dolls, there is an implication that boys "should" like cars and trucks. If girls are given doll houses and tea sets and small furniture for their doll houses, the powerful subconscious (yin) suggestion is that their place is in the home.

Parents and other adults also suggest, even if they don't try to dictate, what clothes are appropriate, what activities their children should engage in, and what future jobs or careers they should aim for. They may not say, "This is what girls or boys do," but the message is clear to the young person.

If the societal conditioning is not in conflict with how children feel about themselves internally, these suggestions, whether explicit (yang) or implicit (yin), will be lived out subconsciously until such a time as they realize that they can make choices of their own.

Most children are yin to their parents and other adults. This means that they take in impressions and embody them. It also means that they are responsive to their parents and seek to reflect in their lives and behavior what they sense their parents want.

One of the common dynamics of the teen years is that children begin to identify with peers. As the need to be liked and approved of by peers grows, adolescents feel the need to break free from the influence of parents. Because teenagers are usually still yin (having turned now to peers for new imprints), they try to be less receptive (less yin) to parental influence. This is experienced by the parents as rebellion whereas it is usually just an attempt by adolescents to exercise some choices (yang) from within the yin. Usually teenagers remain essentially yin to parental influence until adulthood.

If adolescents are primarily identified within as girls or boys, issues of behavior are not likely to be about gender identity. Instead, they will be about boundaries and appropriate behavior within the societal gender definitions. "Boys will be boys" is an expression that means, "that behavior steps outside acceptable boundaries, but it doesn't violate gender identity rules." Somehow stepping outside the boundaries of societal definitions of gender identity is far more offensive and threatening to many adults than simple "bad behavior."

Gender Role Expectations

One of the problems with society's definition of gender identity is that it has been, for a long time, identified with roles people play in society. Consequently gender identity has translated into expectations that women would play the role of nurturing and raising children and men would play the role of wage earner. Women were expected to stay at home and men to go out to work. If women worked, they were expected to do things like teach school, make or sell clothes, clean houses, be secretaries, or become nurses.

During the 20th century, those role-definitions began to change. One impetus was that many women went out of the home to work during World War II because there were jobs that needed to be filled while the men were overseas fighting the war. Many women took jobs in factories, for example, that until then had never been filled by women. When the war ended, not all women wanted to withdraw from employment outside the home.

A second impetus was the Women's Liberation movement. It was started by women who became conscious that gender-specific roles limited their choices and their self-expression. They began to insist that they could do anything men could do, and that they deserved to be paid on a par with men. More and more women went into business and business management, into science and technology, into medicine, and eventually into military service and space travel.

Now that you have some understanding of how the yin and yang work together you can easily discern why, as women asserted themselves (yang), men began to feel freer to express their yin sides. More men went into teaching and nursing. More men stayed home to care for their children. More men became therapists, exercising their yin skills of listening and nurturing.

In the 21st century lines between gender role definitions in Western cultures have pretty much blurred so that both men and women feel free to choose across a broad spectrum of careers and job opportunities without feeling that their identity as a man or a woman is threatened. Equal pay for women has not yet been achieved in the United States, but for the most part women feel their work is of equal value.

Even though gender role definitions vary from culture to culture, and within cultures from time period to time period, it can nevertheless be difficult to feel "I am a woman" or "I am a man" if you do not accept your own society's definitions. However, those who step outside the definitions are the catalysts for societal change. They pay a price for being "different," but they help the overall culture to expand (yin) and become more inclusive (yin).

In the Wrong Body

But what about those whose sense of gender identity leads them to feel they are in the wrong body?

Esoteric traditions have long taught that an evolving spirit incarnates for seven lifetimes in a male body and then for seven lifetimes in a female body. This alternating between genders continues until the spirit achieves a balance of the yin and yang in consciousness. Within that framework, those traditions suggest that someone who is confused about gender identity is probably a spirit who has completed a seven-year cycle and is beginning another in the opposite polarity.

For example, if you spent seven lifetimes in male bodies and were thoroughly identified with embodying the yang polarity, it might be hard to make the transition into a female body at the start of another seven-year cycle. You would know yourself as "male" and yet find yourself in a female body. The confusion might be very painful.

I offer this ancient teaching as one possible explanation of this phenomenon. There are two other possibilities that occur to me. Esoteric traditions teach that when we are ready to incarnate, we are attracted to life circumstances that will serve our further evolution. Supposing you are drawn to a given couple because of many factors that will serve you, such as socioeconomic status, educational opportunities, talents the parents have, belief systems the parents hold, etc. However, as the fetus develops it turns out to be female rather than male, or vice versus, the opposite of the gender you were preparing to embody. This could be a kind of "accident" of birth. You would then have to respond to that uncomfortable circumstance as a way of building your strength as a personality and spirit.

In our time, there is a third possibility. More parents are choosing which gender they want their infant to be. If the parents are not attuned to the incarnating spirit, they could make a "wrong" choice from the point of view of the child.

Even though we do not know for certain why some people feel they are in a body of the wrong gender, we do know that it happens and that the personality and spirit can be very conflicted in that circumstance and suffer a great deal both mentally and emotionally. Modern medical science makes it possible for people to undergo what is called gender reassignment therapy, which often (but not always) includes hormone replacement therapy to modify secondary sex characteristics and sex reassignment surgery to alter primary sex characteristics and provide permanent hair removal for transwomen.

In addition to undergoing medical procedures, transsexual people who go through sex reassignment therapy usually change their social gender roles, their legal names, and their legal sex designation. The entire process of change from one gender presentation to another so that the body reflects the individuals' psychological/social gender identity, that is, their inner sense of self, is known as a "transition." It is of interest to me that in esoteric circles the word "transition" is used to indicate the change we go through at death. Often that change includes a gender change from yang to yin or yin to yang upon reincarnation, so perhaps there is a way in which modern science makes it possible to transition consciously from one sexual identity to another. This could represent another way we are learning to be co-creators.

No Strong Gender Identification
There are also people who do not identify strongly

with either gender. Often these people, when asked "do you feel like a man/woman," will say that they really just feel like a person, or a human being. This does not mean that they do not have a sexual identity, which we will address below, but rather that they don't identify strongly with societal gender definitions or roles.

When we begin to identify with self as spirit, identification with gender usually falls away because in spirit we come to know the two, yin and yang, in one self. We come to know wholeness, or completeness. I hope this book will help you to move in the direction of that balance of yin and yang and that sense of wholeness.

It can be difficult for people who are not strongly identified with gender when there are, for example, societal movements like the Women's Liberation Movement pressuring females to fight for women's rights, or Men's Movements that urge males to champion masculine causes. It is possible to be for equal rights for all humans, but not have strong feelings about gender issues. Such women or men are not really traitors to their gender groups; these are simply not strongly identified with them.

Moreover, many women and men form social groups based on gender identity. Those who have no strong gender identification do not enjoy such gender exclusivity and that can be an isolating factor in their social lives.

Sexual Identity

Just to make matters more confusing, sexual identity, namely the gender with which we want to have sexual relations, does not always line up with gender identity. A woman can feel like a woman but be sexually attracted to other women. A man can feel like a man and yet be sexually attracted to other men. This appears to be a contradiction in terms to those who are sexually attracted to the opposite gender.

We addressed this issue briefly in Chapter Four when speaking of the chemical charge that bodies carry. No one yet knows whether sexual identity can be totally explained by chemistry, but we do know that it is not totally determined by gender. However, the challenge of learning to balance yin and yang energies within self remains the same for everyone.

Moreover, some people have very strong sex drives (very yang) and others do not. The chemical attraction and bonding is strongest in the first year or two of any relationship. That is probably a device by nature that guarantees the formation of a family unit if children are born. When a couple stays together for at least two years based on their strong sexual attraction, they have time to build bonds emotionally, again based on yin and yang interaction, and to develop a history together. Those bonds are more enduring than sexual attraction and provide more stability for the family.

However, if one of the partners has a more powerful sex drive (more yang) than the other, the disparity can cause difficulty in the relationship as time goes on. Currently, such relational problems are usually addressed as if the one whose sex drive is weaker (more yin) has a psychological problem. But this may not be the case at all. In fact, it may have more to do with nature's focus on perpetuating the species. Men continue to produce sperm as long as they live and therefore can continue to procreate. For that reason it is important for them to continue (from nature's point of view) to have the urge to engage in sexual intercourse. Women, on the other hand, have a limited number of eggs and when they are spent, women can no longer reproduce except by implanting a fertilized egg in the womb. Since the latter does not require sexual intercourse, the urge to reproduce is not needed.

Generally speaking, men have a stronger sex drive than women. It seems to go with the yang energy charge in their bodies. As a consequence most men begin as adolescents to brag about their sexual prowess. Whether or not they actually have a powerful drive, it is important to their sexual identity to claim it. If a man's sex drive is less powerful, he may develop feelings of inferiority in his sexual identity, even though he may be attracted to women and function perfectly well as a male in the act of intercourse.

The opposite tends to be true of women. Their sex drive is usually less powerful and less specific (yin), and they seem to talk about their sexuality a lot less than men do. This is in keeping with yin energy, which typically conceals rather than reveals. However, a woman who has a very powerful sex drive may feel that she is "oversexed" and develop psychological problems as a result.

Sexuality is designed to serve the function of procreation, but it is also a powerful way of coming to know the force of love in and through the body. Here I am speaking of love in the most general sense — as a bonding force, as the energy that draws us into union on any and all levels. When we experience that bonding force in our bodies, we call it sexuality. Although it is disturbing to the psyches of many persons when they experience love in their bodies for someone of the same sex, if we recognize that sexual attraction is a specific expression of the more general bonding force of love it can help shift the focus. It is always possible to make choices about how we express love. To experience it (yin) in the body does not compel us to express it (yang) in the body. In terms of our growth in spirit, it is important to know the strong bonding force called love through direct experience on the physical level, in the psyche, and in spirit.

Androgyny

As we humans learn to keep the yin and yang forces in a reasonable state of balance within, androgyny will become more common. Androgyny results from a blending and balance of the two forces. It is often difficult to tell whether an androgynous person is male or female by their outer appearance because the two forces are so perfectly blended that neither predominates. These people have male or female organs, but their sexuality is balanced, meaning that they are able to choose whether to have relations with same sex or different sex partners.

At any given time, there are people moving among us who are quite androgynous. People who are strongly identified with their gender are likely to feel threatened by these people because they don't know how to relate to them. In the future, I am guessing that this phenomenon will become much more common. It is not homosexuality or transsexuality. It is androgyny, a balance of yin and yang within a given individual.

In all these cases and many variations that I have not mentioned, we can see that issues of identity can arouse deep feelings and strong convictions in people. We cannot assume that because people are born into a male or female body they will be strongly identified in their sense of self with that gender, nor can we assume that their sexual identity will conform to their gender identity.

In this exploration I have attempted to lift the whole issue of gender and sexual identity into a broader and less personal perspective where the influence of yin and yang energies can be discerned. This may make it possible to address sexual issues and concerns with more understanding. If people are not dismissed as simply making a personal choice that goes against societal norms it will be easier for them to find their way to greater happiness and fulfillment and for others to accept them as they know themselves.

6

Yin and Yang In Your Psyche

The flow between yin and yang energies in your psyche manifests in the interplay between feelings and thoughts. You will have to observe yourself to discover how this dynamic works in you.

Are you quick to have a feeling response to persons and events? Are those feelings strong and clearly defined? And do you have strong preferences, likes and dislikes? Are you volatile in your feeling expression, tending to blurt out how you feel or to blow up when you are mad about something? And then is the feeling gone, once expressed? If so, you tend to be yang in your emotional life.

Or, are you slow to discover what you feel about persons and events? Are your feelings amorphous and hard to identify? Once you know how you feel about something, do you tend to hold on to the feeling, nursing it, cherishing it, but finding it difficult to express to others? Do you lack strong preferences, likes and dislikes, and yet have difficulty letting go of feelings or preferences once you have identified them? If so, you tend to be yin in your emotional life.

If you fall somewhere in between, do you tend to

be more yang than yin, or more yin than yang? Or do you consider yourself a balance of the two, alternating according to the context or situation you are in? Those who want to function consciously in their lives usually aspire to this ideal of balance.

Generally speaking, those who are yang in their emotional life find it easier to make decisions and to take positions on issues because they are quite clear about how they feel about things. People who have less easy access to their feelings, being emotionally more yin, often need a much longer time to make choices and decisions and may be reluctant to take any position on issues because they are uncertain how they feel about things. They may become dependent on others, or be too easily influenced by others' opinions and decisions, and be overly sensitive to criticism by others.

However, to get a complete picture of the balance of yin and yang energies in your psyche, you also need to look at your thought life. Are you quick to form assessments and make judgments? Do you like to aggressively engage with others on topics that interest you? Do you actively pursue knowledge about and understanding of those things that attract you? Do you like to analyze, categorize and label? If so, you tend to be yang in your thinking function.

Or, are you slow to form an opinion or make a decision because you like to gather as much information as you can? Do you tend to take information in and reflect on it at length, turning it over and over before drawing any conclusions? Are you slow to pass judgment because you tell yourself you may not have all the data? Do you tend to listen far more than you talk when in discussion with others, being careful to hear all sides of an issue before making your own assessment? Do you tend to accept others' opinions and judgments rather than formulate your own? If so, you tend to be yin in your thinking function.

Of course these are generalizations, but as you begin to get a feeling for the balance of yin and yang in your psyche you will find it easier to understand your internal processes and your interactions with others.

Developing the Opposite Polarity

If you tend to be yin in both feeling and thinking, you will find it hard to make decisions and to chart your path through life. Strong feelings (yang) are the key element in formulating a strong purpose in life, in selecting a career or life work, in finding a partner, and in identifying a spiritual path. In addition, clear thinking and discrimination (yang) are essential in the decision-making process. Therefore, if you tend to be yin in both feeling and thinking, you will find it very helpful to develop greater yang qualities and skills so that you can function more decisively. In the beginning it will feel foreign to you to function in yang energy, but you will quickly find a balance that is comfortable for you.

One way to develop more yang in your feeling nature is to practice expressing what you feel just as soon as you become aware and are able to label the feeling. It may take a day or two for you to allow a feeling response to surface in your awareness. Your habit may be to tell yourself that it is too late then to express it. Change that habit. Just as soon as you know what you feel, call or write or go to the person and say, "Remember on Tuesday . . . Well, I felt hurt or angry or deeply touched or compassionate." Don't apologize for taking time to discover the feeling. Just give it expression.

If you are in an interaction when you are asked how you feel, say, "I need some time to process this and I will get back to you." Then be sure to respond as soon as you can.

As you practice this, you will find that you become aware of your feelings more quickly. Soon you will be able to identify feelings in the moment and give them expression right then and there. You will have achieved a balance of yin and yang.

One way to develop more yang energy in your thinking process is to set a limit for yourself on how long you can deliberate something. "I will give myself a day to think about this. Then I must make a choice or a decision." And when you make the choice or the decision, do not allow yourself to change it. Let it be. Giving yourself less time to think about something will force you to develop keener discrimination and to more quickly bring order to the chaos (yin) of thoughts. It will also avoid any spinning that may go on in your thought process, taking you over the same ground many times. Yin thinking is often circular; yang thinking is linear.

If you tend to be yang in both feeling and thinking, you may find that you often make mistakes and mis-judgments because you speak or act too quickly, before having all the facts. You may find that you close the door on relationships or job opportunities because you make snap judgments and only later discover that there were possibilities that you had overlooked. You may also find that you are driven by your mind when it seizes upon an idea or a thought and aggressively pursues it without any conscious direction from you. Or you may find that you get carried away with your feelings until they become destructive to you and/or to others.

To bring forward more yin energy, imagine that you have reins on both your feelings and your thoughts. Use those reins to hold back any expression of feelings or quick judgments and decisions. Once you have hold of the reins and are using your yang energy to restrain yourself, begin to breathe consciously until you can feel an easing of the urgency, or the buildup of pressure. Relax your body. Keep breathing in and out in a rhythmic pattern. Then turn your attention to the situation, the other person, or the event to which you were responding. Concentrate on gathering more data. Expand your view of the situation to see the larger context. Listen to the other person or persons involved. Don't allow yourself to speak or act until you feel completely relaxed. This will bring the balancing yin energy into play.

If you tend to be yin in your feelings and yang in your thoughts, you will discover that most of what you feel is in response to your own thoughts rather than to the world around you. When you take an immediate dislike to someone, it may well be because your thoughts jumped to an instant negative judgment before you had a chance to experience the person. Or when you cannot let go of your anger or resentment, you may find that your thoughts keep returning to the offending action or words and will not allow you to consider any new ways of looking at and feeling about the event or the person.

Practice observing your feeling responses, asking yourself what thoughts you were having that could have imprinted your feelings. Then invite yourself to pay attention to what is actually happening. Do not let your thoughts get ahead of your feelings.

If you tend to be yang in your feelings and yin in your thoughts, it will be important to observe how quickly your thoughts become servants to your feelings. When you feel something, the thoughts will jump to explain and justify with little recourse to actual data from the outside world. You will think that you have good reason to feel as you feel, not because circumstances evoked the feelings, but because your thoughts have put rational fences around your feelings to defend them.

In this case it will be helpful if you acknowledge what you are feeling but do not allow your mind to offer any justifications or rationalizations. Instead, teach your mind to focus on what is actually happening in the moment. For example, if you are feeling rejected, instead of telling yourself all the reasons why you feel this way, look instead to see what actually just happened. Just observe. Then try to develop alternative interpretations to free your mind from the automatic response to the feelings.

A Balance of Yin and Yang

As conscious beings, we want to bring feelings and thoughts into a balance of yin and yang energies so that we can process things in a kind of figure-eight loop. If a thought arises first, we will suspend it until we can touch a feeling that is a direct response to the circumstance or to the thought itself. Only then will we loop back to the thought to see if it aligns with the feeling, and if not, we will think it through again, and then go back to our feelings to test out the new thought.

The reverse would also be true. If a feeling surfaces, we will hold it in suspension until we can make an assessment with our thinking process as to whether the feeling was a response to something actually occurring or if it arose out of habit or reflex. Having examined the feeling with our thinking function we will return to the feeling to find it intensified or ameliorated.

In the beginning this conscious back and forth between thinking and feeling may feel cumbersome, but as you practice you will quickly discover that you become good at it and that you can keep your feelings and thoughts in balance and in perspective with regard to your life circumstances. Both functions are meant to serve you in determining your response to outer events, but often they play against each other in such a way as to ignore or compound the outer.

Feelings help you to determine whether a situation, a course of action, a relationship, or an event will contribute to your growth and well-being or whether it will be detrimental to you. If you do not allow yourself to have a feeling response, you will not be able to act on your own behalf.

Thoughts help you to look at things more objectively, as if from a distance. You can take in the facts and look at the larger picture in which the facts are occurring. You can call to mind your life purpose or your objective in the situation and then bring that to bear on the facts. These things help you to assess whether your feelings are in alignment with your intent.

For example, if your objective is to gain employment and your first feeling response to the person interviewing you is negative, you can go to your thoughts to determine whether this person reminds you of someone else whom you dislike and if that is the root of your feeling. Or perhaps you are just plain nervous and with your thinking function you determine that what you are feeling is really fear based on insecurity, not a response to the personality of the interviewer.

These assessments can be made quickly, making it possible for you to decide whether or not to go on with the interview. If you decide the feelings were not actually to the interviewer, you may continue in the process until you discover what you feel based on the interaction. And again you can assess whether those feelings are aligned with the outer reality. In this case, remembering that your objective is to gain employment will help you to keep your feelings in check until you can determine whether or not this is a position you want to take.

As another example, if your objective is to get to know your daughter's new boyfriend, you will want to suspend both feelings and thoughts, go very yin and remain open and receptive to him until you have enough actual data to inform your response. Then you will want to make your figure-eight loop between feelings and thoughts to make certain that both your feelings and your thoughts are in direct response to the young man and not just to your own beliefs, values, preferences, and prejudices.

Yin energy in the emotions will help you to stay open to new people and places and to adapt and adjust to new circumstances, but you need to go yang in your feelings in order to make decisions. Yin energy in your mind will help you to be flexible and open to new information, but you need yang energy to discriminate between what you want and don't want, what is true and not true, and to take decisive action.

As you observe yourself you may well discover that you respond in the present moment out of habits developed in the distant past. You may go yin so as not to make waves, a self-protective habit developed in a violent or emotionally abusive relationship. The question is whether the current situation is threatening in similar ways, or whether you are just afraid it might be based on past experience.

Or you may go yang because you learned in a past relationship that you could be quickly swallowed up by a controlling outer yang. It is important to discover whether in the current interaction you could remain yin and still maintain your integrity.

Identifying and learning to direct yourself when habits reassert themselves requires a lot of conscious practice, intention, and discrimination but the results are worth the effort. The balance of yin and yang energies in the psyche allows you to make conscious choices about your inner life. That will in turn make it possible to create your outer life reality more consciously and effectively. And equally important, that balance will make it much easier for you to function in your heart center in response to impulses from Spirit, as we will see in the chapter that follows.

7

Yin and Yang In Your Spirit

Spirit is that facet of self in which you feel your connection with the Whole. You will have your own name for that all-encompassing field of energy: God, the Universe, the Life Force, the Power-to-Be-Conscious, or some other term that works for you. It is not important what you call it. It is important to feel and know that you are connected to and with all that is.

In infancy, you related to the body as if it were something that belonged to you, discovering "my" feet, "my" hands, "my" eyes, etc. Then as a small child you learned to recognize yourself *as* the body by looking in the mirror and listening to the comments of others about how you looked and what you could and could not do.

Gradually, through the responses and feedback of others, you learned about your psyche. You became aware of your feelings and thoughts, and you gradually learned that you could have a modicum of control over how you expressed them. As you identified your patterns of responding and as you developed opinions and beliefs about others and the world, you believed, "This is who I am and how I am, and there's nothing I can do about it."

However, sometime in your teen years or early

twenties a new awareness began to dawn. You began to realize that you could "change" yourself. Plenty of self-help books and programs were available and you had had enough experiences to know that you were sometimes your own worst enemy because of patterns you had developed. Habitual ways of acting and reacting may have begun to interfere with relationships and job opportunities. You realized that not only could you change, but you needed to and wanted to.

You may not have realized it then, but that was the beginning of knowing yourself as spirit. It is in spirit that you are able to make conscious choices about how to act and speak and feel and think. It is in spirit that you eventually come to know "I am not just a body, nor am I just a psyche. I am more than both of those." The "more" is what we call spirit. It is an expression of consciousness that can transcend both time and space. It is in spirit that you come to know, rather than just to act, feel, think, or believe.

You may not be very aware of yourself as spirit. Knowledge of that facet of self may be buried in your subconscious memory (in yin), available to you only through intuition. Intuition is the yin polarity of knowing.

However, as you learn to balance the yin and yang forces in body and psyche you will learn how to function through the heart center. The heart center is the balance point in your energy field. It corresponds to the center of the chest. The arms and hands are physical extensions of the heart center and when you stretch them out to the side, you can sense how the heart center energy helps you to balance in your body.

The heart center is also the balance point for the psyche. When feelings are lifted up into the heart and thoughts settle down into stillness, a new capacity opens to you. It is the ability to love unconditionally and to see self, others and the world through eyes of love. In the heart center there is a balance of yin and yang energies. Notice that when you breathe, the heart center expands (yin) and contracts (yang) naturally, as reflected in your chest. If you correlate your awareness with your breath, then when you breathe in you can take in (yin) the energy of everything that surrounds you as well as your own sensations, feelings and thoughts. Then as you breathe out you send (yang) your energy back into the world around you.

Between the in-breath and the out-breath an al-chemical process can occur which transforms everything you have taken in and makes it life-giving. When you first discover this, it is almost like a miracle. If someone is angry at you, spewing negativity, you can breathe in that energy through the heart center. When you release the breath, it is as though all the static has been removed and what you give back to the other person is unconditional love. You can do the same with grief, distress, fear, and any other energy that seems threatening or disturbing. The key lies in focused attention in the heart center so that your feelings and thoughts don't react; instead you channel the energy through the heart and transform it into the binding force of love.

As you learn to love unconditionally by learning to breathe in and breathe out without resistance or obstruction from feelings and thoughts, you will find that you remain balanced in both body and psyche and that you are much more able to make conscious choices about what you feel, think, and do. In this way you begin to experience the nature and essence of spirit. Spirit differs from the psyche in that it is not personal. The heart has no preferences, which are the domain of feelings, and no opinions, which are formed in thought. When you are focused in heart center energy it is possible to gain a larger view of yourself and your life.

The heart center is your access to spirit. There are three important functions to activate in spirit: observing, directing, and creative imaging. Recognizing these three functions helps you to assess the balance of yin and yang throughout your being. By activating and exercising the faculties of spirit, you will become increasingly conscious that you are spirit living in, through, and as a body and psyche.

The Observing Function

You are surely aware that you observe yourself as you move through the day. When you are observing in yin, you are unaware of the process of observing. However, you are able to look back on the activities of the day and remember what you did and said. Not everything, of course, because this was yin observing and much of it will be undifferentiated and unorganized (yin) until you bring it into consciousness (yang). But you will be able to access a lot of it, and if you were put under hypnosis, you could remember nearly every detail.

It is this yin polarity of observing that makes it possible for you to look back over your life and learn from experiences you had before you were aware that you were making choices and taking actions that had long-term consequences. The entire science of depth psychology is based on this yin observing function. What is recorded in memory (yin) from those observations can be called into consciousness (yang) and examined (yang).

When you become aware of the observing function, you can set it in motion consciously. The yang polarity of observing is active and purposeful. In the course of the day, you can observe yourself and make conscious choices about your thoughts, feelings, and actions in the ways we discussed in the two preceding chapters. You will develop keen discrimination, learning to identify what is transpiring in your body and psyche so that you can take conscious direction of them. These are characteristics of yang functioning.

If you have not yet activated the yang polarity of your observing function, this can be a new and exciting challenge for you. In order to **consciously create the reality you live in***, you first need to be conscious of how you are currently creating your reality. It is through the yang polarity of observing that you will make this discovery.

As you are consciously observing yourself, you will also find that it is natural and easy to access memories stored by the yin polarity of the observing function. As you do so, you will find patterns and habits that have formed deep ruts and have prevented you from changing in the ways you want to change. The yang polarity of spirit will expose those habit patterns and make it possible for you to make new choices.

The Directing Function

In the yang polarity of the directing function, spirit motivates you to feel, think, and act in ways that express a higher purpose than what the personality might identify. For example, in your psyche you might desire to be loved and use your thoughts to figure out what actions to take to make others love you. Spirit, on the other hand, might motivate you to expand this objective to a desire to *know* love. This larger objective makes you immediately aware that to know love, you not only need to be loved, but you also need to express love. In this way, you become conscious of your ability to create what you want, rather than feeling that you need someone else to give it to you. If you learn to express love, the law of attraction will call love to you.

In the yang polarity of directing you will activate and empower your personal expression in the world. You will identify and put into words your life purpose, your period purpose and your objectives. These are things you want to develop in yourself so that you can be an integrated, whole being, and so that you can give meaning to all your life experiences.

A Life Purpose is not a specific goal. It is rather a developmental intention that gives meaning to everything you do. When you identify a Life Purpose, it names a deep longing (yin) in you that is powerful enough to keep you motivated until you die. Some examples of Life Purposes are: to serve (respond to the needs of) others; to *be the change I want to see happen in the world***; to embody what I know; to live a life of integrity; to embody unconditional love; to know myself and to my own self be true; to know God; to know Truth; to embody the larger Will.

When you identify a Life Purpose, you seek to align everything you do with that intention even though you know you cannot totally fulfill it in one lifetime. Nevertheless, it is your deepest and highest longing and you seek to live it as fully as you can. Your Life Purpose should be stated in such a way that you can embody it (yin) without depending on other people, not even on their response. And it should be something you can practice everywhere and any time.

A Period Purpose is similar, but it is a more honed (yang) intention that arises in you for a time, usually in response to specific challenges you are facing or because you have discovered something you need to develop if you are to fulfill your Life Purpose. Period Purposes are supportive of the Life Purpose, but they are more specific (more yang). Some examples of a Period Purpose are: to reach out to others; to listen deeply; to practice patience; to suspend judgment; to express gratitude daily; to encourage others; to study the Wisdom Teachings; to speak my truth; to listen inwardly for feelings and intuitions; to act on what I know; to show compassion to those who are suffering; to notice what is; to bring my full presence to every moment.

Again, Period Purposes are stated as active (yang) verbs so that you can do them, you can embody (yin) them, whether or not others support or respond to them.

Objectives are supportive of the Life Purpose and Period Purpose, but are quite specific and very active (very yang). These are things you can practice in almost all situations, such as: to listen; to observe; to express thanks; to notice details; to pay attention; to offer praise; to ask for help; to express myself clearly; to use powerful words; to look people in the eyes.

As you can see, Objectives are not different from Period Purposes, but you might focus on them for a more limited time period, like during a given meeting, while you are at work, while visiting relatives, or when being confronted by a difficult person. In other words, you choose an Objective that is quite pointed in order to stay focused in a specific context and to stay aligned with your Period and Life Purposes. (All yang intentions.)

Finally we come to **Goals**. In the yang polarity of the Directing faculty, we are goal-oriented. Goals are specific targets with end results. We usually lay them out on a time-line. They represent some kind of product or outcome which can be identified by others as well as by self. Some examples of Goals: to lose 10 pounds by summer; to complete the novel I am writing by December; to visit all the national parks in the United States by the time I turn 50; to put all my children through college; to own my own house.

One way Goals differ from purposes and objectives is that you can fail to reach them. You cannot fail in relation to Purposes and Objectives, however. They are stated intentions. When you forget about them or do not embody them, you can either change them or reaffirm them, but nothing is lost in the process. Your overall intention is to grow in consciousness and in skillful living. As long as you are alive you can learn from every experience and continue to expand your consciousness (yin) and hone your life skills (yang). Nothing is lost, even when you fail to reach a Goal.

Also essential to the process of learning and growing is the yin polarity of the Directing function. In the yin polarity you will take in data from the Observing function and receive the imprint of the stated intentions of the yang polarity of your Directing function. Then you will hold all of that information in a container of consciousness and let it gestate. Gradually it will take form as the *how*. Again and again as you identify what you want in life, the question arises, "But how?" The how arises from the yin polarity of the Directing function.

Coming to know how is different from "figuring out" how. In the yin polarity of the Directing function, you need to wait patiently and allow the how to surface from the container in which the facts and the intentions are being held. The how takes shape in subconsciousness (yin). It bubbles up to the surface of your awareness. It "occurs" to you. Often it will surprise you. Always you will feel a kind of agreement move through your whole field, as if body, psyche and spirit are all aligned and saying yes, this is good, this will work.

If you "think" of a how, often you will find that you are trying to convince yourself that it is a good idea. Sometimes your feelings will go into upheaval. Sometimes the body tenses up, as if preparing to resist. However, if you allow the how to surface intuitively (yin), your whole self will be at peace. Often the insight will be followed by a deep sigh, which is like your psyche saying, "yes, thank you." After this intuitive perception surfaces, your objective mind (yang) can help to make the plan more detailed (yang). It can lay out the possible sequence of cause and effect (a very yang way of looking at it). However, it will be important not to allow the mind to question what has surfaced from subconsciousness, because intuition perceives and knows in a much broader and more expansive way (yin). It is more holistic (yin).

When you embody a how (yin) that has surfaced intuitively, you function on a throughline of energy that is powerful, clear and effective. You cannot control or determine the results or the response of others, but you will find deep satisfaction in yourself that you have been true to what you came to know.

The Creative Imaging Function

There is a lot of talk these days about assuming our role as co-creators in the Universe. It is in spirit that we undertake this responsibility.

It is best to begin with your own life, which is why in these chapters we are identifying the yin and yang forces as they are active in your body, psyche, and spirit. As you learn to work with these two polarities you will be able to make the changes you wish to make within yourself. The faculty of spirit you will use is creative imaging. This is how it works.

In the yang polarity, you identify a change you want to bring about. For example, suppose you suffer from insomnia and you want both body and psyche to move past this habit. You need to get very specific, delineating the changes that you want to have come about. This is a yang function. You determine that you want to fall asleep, stay asleep, and awaken rested and refreshed. Get clear about the hour you want to go to sleep and the hour you want to awake. You send this imprint into the yin polarity of the creative imaging faculty.

In the yin polarity, you invite (yin) an image to form in which you can see and feel yourself falling off to sleep easily, sleeping quietly through the night, and awaking at the appointed hour. You see and feel yourself waking up refreshed and rested, eager to move into the day's activities and able to stay alert all day long. You rehearse this image, always feeling it in your body and emotions as you visualize it with your mind.

Then you let go of the image, trusting the yin Directing function to come up with the how that will enable you to bring this reality into being. Focus on this image each morning as you awaken and each evening before you go off to sleep, infusing it with the energy of desire (a yang polarity activity) and fleshing it out in your visualizing with both kinesthetic sensing and emotional responsiveness to the images you are rehearsing (a yin polarity activity).

Keep the creative imaging alive with a steady will (yang) and a nurturing patience (yin). In time you may have intuitions regarding changes that you need to make in your daily routine, in your end of the day activities, or even in such specifics as the pillow you sleep on or how much light is in your bedroom at night. But **have no expectations***** (yin) about the specific hows that may come to you. The important thing is to continue to use creative imaging until you manifest the desired result.

This is a process that can be applied to any change you wish to bring about in yourself. You first need to identify what you want, being specific about the results (yang), and second to register the creative image in your body and feelings as you rehearse it repeatedly morning and evening until it manifests (yin).

If you try this process once or twice and are faithful in practicing, you will come to trust it implicitly. It is the most direct way to create a new reality and bring about change in your life. It is the direct application of an understanding of the yin and yang forces within your personal energy field, utilizing them as keys to effective living.

As you learn to exercise the Observing, Directing, and Creative Imaging faculties of consciousness in both yin and yang polarities, you will be developing in spirit. Spirit manifests as both conscious (yang) and subconscious (yin) functioning. As you cooperate with both aspects of spirit you will come to know that you are spirit, just as you are body and psyche.

*The six Love Principles, one of which is **Create Your Own Reality Consciously**, will help guide you as you learn to live more consciously as spirit. You will find them listed in Appendix Two at the back of the book.*
This is another of the Love Principles: **Be The Change You Want to See Happen in the World.*
***A third Love Principle: **Have No Expectations, but rather Abundant Expectancy.** Find the others in Appendix Two.*

8

Yin and Yang United Within

We have looked at the interaction of yin and yang forces in the body, psyche and spirit, and we have seen that the balanced expression of each force within each facet of self is very important. However, there is another balance that needs to be addressed, the balance among body, psyche and spirit.

We often think of ourselves as limited by, if not determined by, the body or personality. However, once you understand the yin and yang forces you realize that there is a dynamic interaction between the three facets of self and it is that interplay that determines who and what we manifest at any given time .

Your Body and Your Feelings

The body is yin to the psyche. This means that what you feel and think imprints your body and will come into manifestation eventually. The more conscious you become (the more yang in the psyche), the more quickly things will take form on the physical level.

For example, if you have strong feelings about something and you do not express those feelings in words, sounds, tears, laughter, or some kind of action, the energy of the feelings will congest in you. Those unexpressed feelings may result in what is called a common cold, a sore throat, laryngitis, or congestion in the chest.

A woman once told me she was bogged down and unable to make any decisions or changes. She had manifested extremely bloated legs, as if the water of the "bog" had settled there, making it hard for her to take any steps on her own behalf, both literally and metaphorically. A man once expressed, "I can't stand this" and within days his legs gave way and he could no longer stand or walk without support.

The body often manifests things in this metaphorical way, as if what is experienced on the emotional level translates into the physical and we recognize it through expressions such as a stiff neck (for stubbornness or resistance), an aching back (when feeling burdened), heart trouble (when experiencing grief or relational pain), and so forth.

I do not mean to suggest that all physical conditions are caused by unexpressed emotions. That is definitely not the case. Environmental factors affect us all; genetics play their part; and what we eat and drink and how much we exercise (or don't) have an influence on our physical well-being.

However, it is important to recognize that emotions can and do influence the body when they are not expressed in a timely and effective manner. One way to discover whether your feelings have imprinted your body is to listen to how you talk about your experiences. "She makes me sick!" is a statement meant to be metaphorical, but the body may make it literal. Or, "What a pain in the neck he is!" may be reflected in your neck.

"Those people make my skin crawl" may show up as a skin condition. And so it goes.

The body is yin to what we feel. Imagine what you can do once you are aware of how the psyche affects the body, yang to yin. You can consciously call up feelings of joy, gratitude, happiness, humor and contentment and then watch your body manifest health and well-being. It is not enough to think about how grateful you are, or to remind yourself mentally what a good life you have. You have to infuse your feelings with life force by breathing into them and giving life to them throughout your body. Let your face express the feelings. Make sounds of contentment. Respond to humor with belly laughs. Breathe into your heart center and swell up with gratitude and joy. Find ways to express those good feelings to others with genuine enthusiasm. Your body will respond with relaxation, sound sleep, and good health.

The Body and Thoughts

Fortunately, your thoughts are not as powerful as your feelings in affecting your body, at least until you begin to function more consciously. I say fortunately, because if you observe your thoughts you may notice an astonishing amount of negativity. This may be partly because you have been imprinted by negativity expressed by friends, relatives and the media. It may also be due to your own inclination to look on the dark side and to fear the worst. If your body absorbed (yin) all of that negativity, you would be very ill indeed. Fortunately, most thoughts don't have much power because you do not awaken much feeling in response to them. Therefore they do not make an imprint on the body.

Nevertheless, thoughts do affect the body when they activate (yang) a feeling response (yin) which then impresses (yang) the body (yin). For example, if you have an important meeting coming up and you begin to worry about it, thinking about all that could go wrong and what will happen if you don't do well, you may well arouse (yang) anxiety (yin). The anxiety may evoke (yang) a response (yin) in the body, like a headache, an upset stomach, intestinal gas, or overall tension and stress.

However, you can also learn to use your thoughts to bring about positive responses in your feelings and body. "Self-talk" can support your Purpose and Objectives rather than undermine your best intentions. For example, after preparing for the important meeting you could remind yourself: "I am well-prepared. I have made this kind of presentation before; I can do it again. I just need to breathe deeply, stand up straight, and speak loudly and clearly." Such inner conversation directed at yourself will evoke (yang) feelings of confidence; your body will respond (yin) with calm strength.

The most important thing is to be aware that *the psyche is yang to the body.* Therefore, it is important to monitor your thoughts and feelings if you want your body to be healthy.

Your Psyche and Spirit

As you expand your conscious awareness and develop the faculties of spirit, you will increase your ability to create more consciously your reality in body and psyche. Spirit is yang to the psyche, and because the psyche is yang to the body, you can set in motion a positive and healthful chain reaction.

You will begin by exercising your Observing faculty to help you to identify the effect your feelings and thoughts are having on your body.

Your Directing function will help you to get clear about what you *want* to create in body and psyche and what you can do to fulfill those Objectives.

But most important will be the utilization of your Creative Imaging ability. Once you are clear that you want to make changes in body and psyche, you can begin to develop a clear image of the end result you desire. You will need to watch for any competing beliefs held in the psyche that will counteract the images you are developing. And you will need to identify, express and release the energy of feelings that do not support the change. Here is an example of the process I am describing.

In my Observing faculty I noticed, when I turned 70, that I was tuned into a whole array of beliefs about what happens to us as we age. Most of these were convictions widely held in our culture, such as: we grow weaker; we don't see or hear as well; we develop osteoporosis; our balance is not as keen; we become forgetful; we become fearful of or resistant to change. The list could go on, but you get the point. These beliefs were reinforced by health practitioners who tended to respond to any concerns I had with, "Well, as we age . . . " or "You're getting older, you know."

Turning to my Directing function, I sought to identify what I wanted to do with the rest of my life. I realized I could live another 25 years. That is a very long time, and I want to use the time well. My Life Purpose is to live the Will consciously. I then adopted several Period Purposes: to honor and respect the aging process as one phase in the cycle of life in the body; to expand my awareness of the constantly changing and renewing energy around and within me; to develop my ability to register finer and finer frequencies of energy; and to bring my full presence to each here/now moment.

I then identified some powerful Objectives that would help me to fulfill my purposes. Some of them are: to continue my study of physics; to continue my study of the Wisdom Teachings; to expand the scope of my meditations; to pay attention to changes in energy in the environment around me as I move through each day and to respond to those changes; to respond in energy to what I register in others; to give of myself, of my insight, understanding and wisdom, as I move through each day; to practice speaking a foreign language each day; and to travel in new cultures and environments each year.

Then, addressing the specific concern about what changes I wanted to bring about in body and psyche, I set about the task of changing my beliefs. I reasoned: If this is an energy world and energy is constantly being renewed, why do I assume that body and psyche will disintegrate as I age? Instead, it seems reasonable that both body and psyche could be in a continual process of sloughing off the old and bringing in the new. Instead of being concerned that aches and pains are a sign of aging, I decided to consider them signs of change. Pain in a joint indicates that change is occurring. Pain in a muscle is a sign of toxins being discharged. In each case, I breathe into them and through them to help release the cells that are dying and to bring in new life-force for renewal and regeneration. In other words, I decided to consciously help my body to deal with changes taking place, instead of viewing each symptom as an indicator of a downward slide into "old age."

During this time I heard others lamenting about their loss of memory, referring often to "senior moments." I acknowledged that my pace of engaging with life has slowed and that I don't multi-task well any more. I decided to welcome these changes as opportunities to live more fully in the here and now and to savor each moment of life. I also affirmed that because there is a lot of data stored in my memory, it takes a little longer to find specific information now than it did when I was 25. I continue to trust my mind to function at its optimum. When I can't remember a name, I go yin to the process, waiting patiently for the information to be brought forward into my conscious awareness. Memory is, after all, a yin function and I have learned I can trust my mind, even if it takes a little more time to retrieve something than it did in the past. In these ways and others, I am affirming the changes occurring in my psyche and expanding (yin) my appreciation (yang) for all I have learned and experienced over the years.

Finally, I went to my Creative Imaging process. I held an image of Light infusing my entire energy field, illumining blocked energy that needs to be moved and providing life-giving force for regeneration and renewal in both body and psyche. I envisioned my body as healthy, balanced, limber, strong, and full of life-force. I imagined my feelings as vibrant, responsive, and full of passion for life. And I saw my mind as agile, flexible, quick to absorb new information, able to retrieve vast amounts of material from memory, and responsive to my Directing function. This latter is essential if I am to quiet the thinking process when I wish to open to intuitive perception.

Each time I review my creative images at the beginning and end of each day, I breathe deeply into my desire to have a life-filled and responsive body and psyche to serve me in this final quarter of my lifetime.

I am now 72 and I feel full of vital energy in my body. My chronic allergies have cleared up. A chronic cough is gone. Work with a chiropractor who shares my conviction that my body can regenerate is correcting postural distortions that created pain in my arms and upper back. I am focused on a specific creative image of the regeneration of the discs and nerves in my cervical vertebrae so that nerves that have been impinged for years can resume their normal functioning. My chiropractor gives me constant encouragement and direction (yang functions), for which I am very grateful. I am sleeping well and my body is strong and flexible. Learning Tai Qi has improved my balance.

I continue to be nourished by relationships and my spiritual studies and meditation so that my psyche is at peace. And recreational and cultural activities add nourishment and balance for my psyche.

That reminds me to say that it is essential to accompany Creative Imaging with positive actions that support and promote the manifestation of the desired outcome. Eating right, exercising regularly, and getting good sleep support the body's process of renewal. The psyche is supported by nourishing contact with other people, by fine music and other arts, by reading and study, and by relaxing entertainment. However, it is the sustained impact of spirit that guides and directs the changes taking place in body and psyche. **Spirit is yang to psyche and body.**

The Balance of Yin and Yang in Self

Until the yang spirit is brought into your conscious awareness, it cannot be a partner for the yin psyche and body. Therefore there will be a long period of time when you remain identified with the psyche, functioning as if you are the personality, while beginning to acknowledge the potential that the yang spirit represents. You may feel like you "have" a spirit, and you will begin to reach to it, ask of it, and ask from it, but for some time your awareness of it will not be strong enough to make it a full partner with the psyche.

Then there comes a shift. You will begin to know yourself as spirit. At that point your consciousness of spirit will be sufficiently developed for you to express its yang force in relation to the yin psyche and to have it as a full partner with the yin.

You identify with the psyche first; then you begin to recognize the spirit that was always there. Gradually you develop a relationship between spirit and psyche, and eventually a union between spirit and psyche is the result.

The wisdom traditions teach us that spirit does not exert control over the psyche; rather, it offers direction and guidance. You always have the option to refuse spirits guidance and to make another choice in personality. For a long time you will continue to respond to values and beliefs and shoulds and oughts that were learned from others. As you grow in consciousness, you will seek to develop cooperation between the two, rather than rebelling in personality against the spirit or attempting to exert power over the psyche as if from spirit.

In early stages of the development of the faculties of spirit, the personality may not be very open to direction from spirit. The psyche is used to being the yang force in relation to the body. It is, in effect, used to running things for the individual.

Before the spirit is fully recognized by you, you will register guidance from spirit through symbols, stories, and metaphors in the form of dreams and intuitions. These are unconscious (yin) methods of communication between psyche and spirit. But eventually there can be a much more conscious interaction and relationship in which you are aware in personality of what spirit is asking of you. Then you have to decide if you are going to cooperate in psyche or not.

Perhaps you can remember times when you were aware of promptings from spirit but you didn't follow them. Later you said, "I knew I should not have done that, but I did it anyway." or, "I felt strongly I should call him but I didn't." As your sense of self as spirit is developing, you will be aware of a tug and pull, a back and forth, between psyche and spirit. Sometimes psyche goes yin to spirit but often it does not.

As your recognition of the yang spirit emerges, you will begin to reach to the personality with compassion and love, and the personality will respond with a desire to unite with spirit. When you come to know yourself *as* spirit, you will reach to embrace the psyche and make it one with you. You will develop a love of and for self, both in personality and spirit. Eventually a union occurs and psyche and spirit function as one rather than two.

The union of psyche with spirit has long been symbolized in esoteric circles by the six-pointed star, which is composed of two triangles that have merged. The triangle that points upwards represents the yang force, or spirit. The triangle that points down represents the yin force, or psyche. Together they represent one individual in whom the yin and yang energies are balanced and working cooperatively in creative expression.

To experience such an inner union, sometimes called the Inner Marriage, is to know a deep inner peace. Decisions can be made and carried out with no inner conflict. Purposes and Objectives held in spirit are harmoniously lived out through psyche and body. Energies are balanced in the heart and it is effortless to express unconditional love.

The potential to form a perfect union with another, a union of body, psyche and spirit, becomes available to you when you have achieved the Inner Marriage of yin and yang.

9

Yin and Yang
In the Creative Process

In the best of all possible worlds, everyone would be adept at embodying the archetypal yin and yang energies in all their interactions. When the two forces are functioning properly, they are equally powerful and completely interactive and cooperative. The yang seeks out the yin; the yin welcomes the yang. The yin seeks to magnetically attract the yang; the yang responds with eagerness to give the gift of an imprint. This is the archetypal relationship between the two forces.

However, sometimes the yin and yang energies are stifled in their expression and they become dysfunctional. Our interactions then become complicated, confusing and nonproductive. Our self-esteem may suffer in such circumstances and we may not learn how to create the lives we desire.

The Creative Process

A creative process begins as the yin energy eagerly awaits an imprint from the yang force. Yin knows its potential to give birth to creations on all levels, physical, emotional, mental and spiritual, and it waits in abundant expectancy for the impetus to come, for it cannot begin the creative process without the yang stimulus. On the physical level, the yin might say, "I want to get pregnant." On the emotional level, "I am waiting for inspiration." On the mental level the phrase might be, "When I get an idea, I will begin." On the spiritual level the yin might feel, "I am willing to do what is wanted." In other words, the yin acknowledges that it will be a nurturing vessel for the new.

The yang force is a partner in this creative process. When the energy surges within it as an urge to have intercourse, it actively seeks the receptive yin. The urge to give the gift of its life-giving seed on the physical level, however, is only one form of intercourse. When the yang fills up with inspiration, when it is bursting with a bright idea, when it swells with emotional affirmation and encouragement, or when it senses the urgency of knowing what is wanted from it in the larger picture of things, it cannot bring anything into being without an inviting, welcoming and actively receptive yin. In other words, the yang is an enthusiastic partner in search of its mate.

As individuals, we experience this dynamic within ourselves. We breathe into the empty creative womb and experience our eagerness for the new. The creative womb is in the spirit and psyche rather than in the physical body. It is an energetic space that is full of life-potential and deep feeling. We prepare ourselves in yin energy to receive and respond to the stimulus that will come. We feel a magnetic energy in the psyche that seeks to draw to itself a vital yang force from spirit. Or, we have a strong desire on the emotional level to attract an idea from the mental level. Or, we feel a physical magnetism that seeks to catch the attention of a yang body.

In the yang polarity, we are alert to energies that awaken within us and stir us to take some action. These energies are exciting, stimulating, energizing, and highly motivating. We are eager to share them, but we know they must take some form before we can do that. For that, we need the yin. If we talk about an idea or inspiration before we have held it in our creative womb, the seed may die. The insight, inspiration, or idea must be held in that expectant container (our yin energies), nurtured and fed on our passion for the new, until it has taken sufficient form to be given expression (yang) in thought, word and action.

Any creative process is an active exchange of energies between yin and yang. Imagine business partners who are brainstorming how to grow their business. Both are galvanizing their inner yang forces as they exchange ideas. The question is, do they also activate their inner yin? If they do not, they simply throw ideas back and forth, bouncing off each other. Nothing will come of any of them. A creative exchange requires that an idea be received and held for a time (yin). It must be explored and fleshed out, metaphorically speaking, in order to see where it would take them. Once that is done, another idea can be explored in a similar fashion. If the process is done in this way, both partners will have the satisfaction of being creative.

Another kind of creative partnering occurs when one of the partners, let's say a composer, writes a piece of music as an expression of an inner creative process. Then a lyricist puts words to the music. Or, an author writes a book and then an artist illustrates the text with original drawings. Or, a playwright develops a drama, a director stages it with actors who bring it to life, a costume designer clothes the actors, and a scene designer creates the set. All of these people bring their inner creativity, which is a balance of yin and yang, to bear on a joint creative project that, hopefully, will bring delight to many people.

In many creative projects the yin and yang functions are alternated in a kind of chain reaction. Homeowners decide to remodel their house. In their inner creative process they have images (yang) of what they want to create and they have strong feelings (yin) about those images. They develop a powerful creative image of their remodeled home in a dynamic back and forth of yin and yang energies between them.

They then hire an architect who sits down with them and listens (yin) to their ideas and feelings. He goes away and draws a plan (yang) which he brings back to the homeowners. The homeowners consider it (yin) and give their approval (yang).

The next step is for the homeowners to hire (yang) a contractor who accepts (yin) the architect's design and the homeowners' creative image. He brings together (yang) a group of workers who can actually do the remodeling (yin). As the workers carry out their various functions, they exchange yin and yang energies with each other in a totally cooperative way.

The result is a remodeled house that gives creative satisfaction to the homeowners, the architect, the contractor and all the workers.

Dysfunctional Yin and Yang
Let's consider what happens, however, when the yin

is dysfunctional in some way. A yin that feels unworthy is not likely to seek to interest the yang force. She may fear that she will not be able to bear children or produce anything creative on any level. If she does not send out her magnetic energies, no yang will be attracted to her. Internally, if you do not feel creative, no ideas or inspirations will be forthcoming in you.

The result is a self-fulfilling prophecy. The yin, feeling unworthy, fails to magnetize the yang force. As a consequence she feels useless and a failure as a yin. If the yang should force himself on her, the yin will feel violated, victimized, and used. She will not receive the yang thrust as a gift and she will feel the task of nourishing, bringing forth, and sustaining the new (the "child") as a burden rather than a privilege. In our inner process, this kind of reaction in the yin usually occurs when you feel required to "produce." So you do, not because you are inspired (yang) but because it is expected of you. Yin may begrudge creating anything under those circumstances and may feel resentful even though productive.

If the yang force reaches out and is ignored, it will begin to lack self-confidence and will find it more difficult to initiate and to offer its gifts of creativity. If it approaches the yin again and is rejected, it will begin to feel impotent. Once again, this may be self-fulfilling.

This is something that happens in our inner process more than we realize. We have an idea or an inspiration but we are afraid we will not be able to bring it into being (this is yin feeling unworthy), so we let the idea die. Then the next time we get an idea, we will have even less confidence in it, feeling that it is probably no good (yang feeling impotent). In the first instance, it was yin that was feeling unworthy, but the fact that the yin force did not receive the yang imprint made the yang start doubting itself.

Many times we interrupt the creative process without meaning to. Someone offers a suggestion (yang) and we are in a hurry, so we don't really take it in (dysfunctional yin). Instead we brush it off. Subconsciously, the one who offered the suggestion may have less confidence in yang energy the next time an opportunity arises. It is a simple thing to acknowledge the suggestion and say "May I think about that and get back to you?"

Or, sometimes we rush in with yang energy without considering that the yin may not be ready to receive us. If the yin force does not feel respected, or feels violated, it may find it more difficult to trust the next yang impetus.

Internally, it takes self-discipline to keep these creative energies flowing. Sometimes an idea or inspiration comes at the most inconvenient time: in the middle of the night, while you are driving your car, as you are about to participate in a conference call, when company is about to arrive, etc. It only takes a moment to acknowledge the idea internally, making a mental note of it. Then, at the earliest opportunity it is important to write it down so that it is fixed in your creative womb. If you do not receive it in that way (yin), your yang force will be weakened by your inattention. Creativity does not recognize convenience.

Extended Creative Processes

There is another aspect of the creative process that we have not talked about. It is what we might call the long haul. Many creative undertakings have to be sustained over long periods of time. Both the yin and the yang need to stay engaged until the process is brought to completion. Take this book as an example.

Back in 1985 I received an inner directive from spirit (yang) to write a series of books on the Wisdom teachings. I responded in yin willingness and within a very short time, I wrote and published an introduction to the series. That was an initial product of a creative urge.

However, life then intervened and it was about ten years before I began to write the second book in the series. My inner yang force had catalyzed the process, but if it had not stayed attentive and involved, the seeds held in my creative womb might have died. Each time I went within to sense whether the inspiration was still alive, I would feel a quickening, a life-giving impulse from the yang.

The yin, on the other hand, had to have incredible patience, strength and endurance to see the process through to completion. I had manifested one book, but there were more to be given birth. In order to hold the embryos in the creative womb, my inner yin had to be willing to have faith that the books would get written. This took trust in the strength of the initial creative urge as well as in its own ability to give the books form.

In all creative processes the yang plays a very important supportive role. Some of the functions it serves are to encourage, inspire, praise, admire, offer suggestions, correct, guide, direct, and express trust, confidence and appreciation. These are energizing functions. They renew the energy of the original thrust for the process the yin is engaged in, even though that process is relatively hidden in the inner creative womb.

In my case, each time I returned to the inspiration to bring forth a new book, the energy was still alive. The current book is the fifth and final in the series. I have had to infuse my personality with a lot of encouragement from spirit to complete an energy thrust that began over 20 years ago.

I feel confident you have had a similar experience. You have the brilliant idea (yang) to clean the garage. You are enthusiastic about it (yang) and willing (yin). Then you begin. It is so much more work than you anticipated that it takes an incredible amount of time. Moreover, there are endless decisions (yang) to be made about what to save and what to throw away. It is easy to sag into weariness rather than to sustain your energy (yin) until the project is completed. It is helpful if, during the time you are hard at work (yin), someone drops by to say, "Great job!" That's a yang function that I like to call cheer leading. It infuses us with new energy (yang), making it easier to go on (yin).

I'm sure you can think of many occasions when you undertook something and would have quit in the middle of the creative process if someone hadn't come along to tell you they knew you could do it, to praise you for what you had accomplished thus far, to thank you for your hard work, to admire what you were doing, or even to make suggestions that helped you to finish the project successfully. All of those contributions were yang force infusing you with energy to sustain your effort in yin.

If, however, the yin is not sought out by the yang in the beginning, it will feel unworthy and useless. If the yang forces itself upon the yin without being invited, the yin will feel violated and victimized. If the seed implanted by the yang is not fertile, the yin will feel like a failure. And if the yin is not supported, encouraged and appreciated by the yang as she does her work of manifestation, she will feel abandoned and used.

A yin force that feels unworthy, useless, a failure, violated, victimized, abandoned and/or used, will find it difficult to receive as a gift the thrust of the yang in new interactions, and will feel the task of bringing forth, nourishing and sustaining the new (the "child") as a burden rather than a privilege. Carl Jung labeled this dysfunctional yin within us as the negative anima. It is born of lack of attention and appreciation by the yang force, or of the frustration caused by a lack of vital force in the seed-pattern implanted in her womb.

If you find yourself feeling any of these characteristics of the dysfunctional yin, be aware that you need to fire up your inner yang to motivate and support the yin. The cheer leading function of yang is especially important here, reassuring yourself that you can bring forth whatever is needed, that you are powerful and creative and that you will be there for yourself, encouraging and guiding yourself without flagging.

Sometimes it is the yin force that needs to encourage the yang. Supposing you are working on an innovation at work that could bring about a positive change that would not only make a lot of money but make life much easier for many people. However, though you are confident the idea will work, you can't quite get the design right. Yin energy is essential, whether from within yourself, or from others in your office. You need a nonjudgmental environment in which you feel safe to keep trying. You need to be encouraged by your inner yin or others around you who say they have confidence in you, they know you can do it, who remind you of past achievements, who tell you they are ready to help in any way they can. These are all yin functions, and they make it possible for yang to sustain the effort when the going gets rough.

On the other hand, if the yang is surrounded by dysfunctional yin energy it will not receive this kind of support. If it is ignored, it will begin to lack confidence. If it is not valued, it will feel impotent. If what the yang offers is not welcomed by the yin, the yang will feel rejected. If the yang contribution is not invited by the yin, the yang will feel the need to use force to imprint the pattern, and will resent the yin for lack of cooperation. If the yang idea or inspiration or seed of new beginning does not bear fruit, the yang will feel distrustful of the yin in future interactions, feeling it was the yin that failed him.

A yang force that lacks confidence, that feels rejected and impotent and is resentful and distrusting of the yin, will find it difficult to initiate in future interactions. It will hesitate to offer its gift of creativity, and it will be reluctant to encourage and support the yin. In effect, the yang will become dysfunctional. This can happen within us as well as between us and others. Carl Jung labeled this dysfunctional yang the negative animus. It is often viewed as an intruder, a tyrant or an oppressor. In all cases it is born of the lack of being received, welcomed and cherished by the yin force.

If you feel the characteristics of the dysfunctional yang, you now know how to bring forward your yin energy to invite the yang to try again, reassuring it that you will receive its ideas and work with it to bring them into manifestation. In yin energy, you need to make it safe for the yang to fail and try again. You need to express patience when new undertakings don't go well. You need to trust yourself and the creative forces that move through you. You can help your inner yang force to regain its power and thrust.

Antagonistic Forces

When either the yin or the yang becomes dysfunctional, the two forces that are archetypically cooperative and productive can become antagonistic. Either of the forces can feel it is the victim of the other rather than an equal partner in a union. Either can become death-dealing rather than life-giving. Both will resist rather than cooperate and try to control rather than being lovingly responsive. Yang controls through force and criticism, which is very direct. Yin controls through manipulation, which is hidden and indirect.

These dysfunctional archetypal forces become angry and hostile rather than deeply feeling and vulnerable, and fearful rather than eager and trusting. They will both be self-protective rather than tender and solicitous. Rather than showing care, attention and concern for the other and being eager to know the other intimately, they will be distrustful, watching out for their own self-interests. And instead of offering themselves openly and giving freely of themselves, they will become withholding and stingy.

Perhaps you have experienced persons who have manifested one or the other of these dysfunctional archetypal creative forces. If so, you know that it is very difficult to work with them. And if one or the other, or both, of your inner forces has become dysfunctional, you will find that your life does not go well and you are not able to be very successful in any of your endeavors or relationships.

This is all the more reason to become acquainted with the yin and yang and to bring them into functional balance in your own life.

Daily Life as a Creative Process

We often think of creativity as being expressed in a specific project or action. Actually, however, all of daily life is a creative process for the conscious person.

You start the day by remembering that you have the power to **create your own reality consciously***, so you bring into focus your Life Purpose, your Period Purpose and your Objectives for the day. These are yang expressions of Spirit that set the tone for all your activities. In yin energy you then open to discover how you will give life to these intentions.

You prepare yourself mentally by looking at your calendar to see what activities are scheduled. In yang energy, you organize the day, setting priorities and co-ordinating time schedules, if that is important. Then in yin energy, you invite your mind to remind you of that schedule as you move through the day.

Emotionally it is very helpful to choose, in yang energy, what feelings you want to awaken, and in yin energy to breathe life into those feelings so that you can feel them throughout your energy field.

Physically you will want to get your body moving with yin stretches and yang exercises so that you are fully alive on all levels.

This done, you are ready to move into your day with **no expectations, but abundant expectancy.***

Recently I began a day with these preparations. My Life Purpose has long been to do the larger Will. My Period Purpose was to live in gratitude, in joy, and in compassion all day every day. And my specific Objective was to support and celebrate my brother who was to be awarded a peace prize that weekend. I was to fly to New York City for that event. Air reservations had been made months earlier and other plans and arrangements were all in place for the five days in New York. There were a few last minute details to attend to before leaving for the plane.

I was excited about going. I felt happy and grateful to be able to attend this big event. I had watched the morning news while doing my morning stretches and exercises and had opened wide in yin energy to take in the weather report, which predicted severe weather on the East Coast. I made a mental note to call the airline before leaving for the airport to see if my flight was on time.

I went out for my morning swim. When I came back in for my shower, I noticed a message was waiting for me. The call had been from Southwest Airlines telling me that my plane had been canceled due to weather. Feelings of disappointment swept over me as I took in the information in yin energy. I immediately shifted into yang, calling the airline to see if I could reschedule the flight for the next day. Again I went yin to the news that there were no openings the next day.

Now my disappointment was extreme. I could feel my energy draining away. My mind began to race in yang energy, searching for alternatives to save the day. I was observing myself and knew I needed to activate my directing function to bring new order to the day. I consciously expanded in yin energy to make space for my disappointment while I moved into yang action to cancel reservations and notify people of the change in plans.

After eating breakfast and unpacking my bags, I sat down to take stock of my situation. It was hard to acknowledge that ***problems are opportunities*** * because of my deep disappointment, but I knew it is always true. So what was my opportunity? What new reality could I create? Gradually I recognized that four and a half completely open days lay ahead of me. My calendar was completely empty. This was a rare occasion.

My original Objective had been to support and celebrate my brother. I knew I could continue to do that from afar, but now I added another Objective, which was to focus on my own creative endeavor, with the goal of getting a book ready for the printer. Once I had identified this new Objective I regained my focus (yang) and my energy began to flow again. I was still disappointed about missing the award ceremony, but I awakened excitement about having uninterrupted time to work on my book.

For the next four days my conscious attention (yang) was on the completion of the book. On the sub-conscious level (yin), my mind was working on possible ways to compensate for the lost opportunity to share something meaningful with my brother. At odd moments, alternatives popped to the surface of my awareness and I put them in a holding pattern (yin) for later decision-making. Meanwhile I utilized the free time in a productive and creative way while rejoicing in reports from New York City about how the weekend was going for my brother and his family.

Even when we make careful plans for how our days will unfold, unexpected things can intervene. When that happens, we can choose either to feel like a victim of events, powerless and thwarted, or we can redirect our energies. The creative forces are still available to us, but we have to choose a new channel into which they can flow.

Let me offer another kind of example of life as a creative process. Sometimes we are presented with a challenge of a different kind. Several years ago I began to have a lot of pain in my right leg. This set in motion about a three-year series of exchanges of yin and yang energy between me and a whole series of health professionals.

I first reached out to my chiropractor, telling her about the pain and asking her, in yin, if she could help me. I yielded to her treatments (yin) while reporting to her (yang) what seemed to help and what didn't. After several months of regular appointments, she suggested I go to another practitioner who had been able to help people with muscular pain. I trusted my chiropractor and was willing to follow her suggestion (yin).

Marcia (not her real name) had developed her own style of physical therapy. I didn't like her manner of relating to me, but I remained in yin out of respect to my chiropractor and out of my own need for help with the pain in my leg which was growing worse.

After only two sessions, Marcia became completely frustrated with me, telling me I was refusing to let go of the tension in my right leg. She told me she thought it was psychological and recommended I go to a guy who did hypnotherapy. I could feel my resistance rising, but

I didn't want my dislike of Marcia to interfere with my healing process. So I went twice to the hypnotherapist, with no change in the pain level or any other level that I could discern.

During that entire year I was also working at home with relaxation and attention to pain, trying to find my way within myself to a resolution of the problem. I observed myself with keen awareness so that I could give thorough descriptions (yang) to the health professionals to guide the application of their skills. I disciplined myself to have patience (yin) and to cooperate fully with each professional I saw.

My next yang thrust was to consult my family doctor. He sent me for an MRI, which showed that I did not have compressed nerves in my lower back that would be causing all this pain. In response, my doctor, whom I also trust, referred me to a physical therapist. I responded in yin compliance. I liked the physical therapist, who tested the range of movement in my right hip and assured me that my hip was not the problem. He gave me hands on therapy each time I went, stretching the leg every which way, and his assistants gave me lots of exercises to do. The pain persisted.

So I moved into yang energy again and went to a pain clinic. They did decompression therapy to relieve the pressure on my lower back (which even *their* MRI indicated I did not have) and recommended physical therapy at their clinic, which I went to only three or four times because it was even less effective than the first physical therapy I had done.

I studied Zen techniques of pain management, which were a lovely balance of yin and yang energies, but the pain grew more intense. Once again I moved into yang energy. A friend told me of another physical therapist who is also a Yoga Master. I hoped I could work better with him. My family doctor gave me the referral I requested and in fact Matt was able to teach me how to alleviate a lot of the most intense pain.

However, finally I was so tired of being in constant pain that made it difficult to walk, sit, stand, and sleep, that I returned to my family doctor and said, "I think we should x-ray my hip." We did and when we looked at the x-rays he said, "No wonder you have been in so much pain. Your cartilage is completely gone and you are walking with bone on bone."

I found it difficult to believe that not one of the therapists I had seen nor my family doctor had ever suggested a hip x-ray. Perhaps it was because all the pain I experienced was in my leg, not in my hip, or perhaps because I had kept my leg and hip socket limber with many years of stretching and exercise. But the fact is that in the end it was my intuition that called for a hip x-ray.

The next step was to find an orthopedic surgeon. By now I was fully into my yang energy, managing my own care. The first surgeon I saw was one of the most recognized in our valley. His waiting room walls were covered with awards and pictures of satisfied patients. However, when he finally came in to meet and examine me, he spent about seven minutes with me. He said I was a good candidate for surgery and told me to talk to his assistant about scheduling. I walked out, knowing I would not be back.

I sought other recommendations. When I saw the surgeon I chose, she spent an hour with me. She asked me questions about my diet, my exercise routine, and my mental and emotional states. She asked if I had a support system that would see me through the recovery from surgery. Only at the end of this extensive period of getting to know me did she examine my hip. She had required a series of x-rays before she would see me and she looked at them with me, explaining what the problem was and how she would recommend replacing the hip joint.

I had done extensive research online (yang) before going, so I was prepared to ask her many questions. She took time to respond to each question in depth. She listened to me (yin) and responded fully (yang). I listened to her (yin) and probed with more questions (yang). I came away from the appointment feeling that she cared about me as a whole person and would be a careful and skilled surgeon. That proved to be the case.

My biggest learning from that long process was that sometimes being pain tolerant, which I am, is not a good thing. I persisted with therapies that didn't help and trusted specialists to tell me what was wrong. In the end it was my intuition that said, "Let's x-ray the hip." I don't know how long it would have taken for one of these specialists to suggest my hip as the problem, but perhaps I would have taken the initiative sooner to insist we find out what was causing the pain if I had not been able to tolerate the pain.

I let go of an underlying belief that suffering pain serves some purpose beyond being an alarm mechanism. I think the belief stemmed from some concept of martyrdom in my Christian upbringing. I learned to listen to my body, to trust that it knows when something is wrong, and to take action in response to those messages.

I learned how important it is to listen to my intuition even when so-called specialists are guiding my care. I learned that I can trust the body's capacity to heal and restore its equilibrium when it has the right support. I developed a deeper trust in the body and its innate wisdom.

The end result of nearly five years of pain and healing is that I have a new hip that works beautifully and I am able to walk, run, sit, stand, and sleep with no pain. I am grateful each day for the privilege of a leg and hip that serve me so well. And I am aware that this creative process only worked because I was a full, active, and equal participant with the various health professionals. I maintained my sense of responsibility for my own healing and solicited assistance from those who had skills I didn't have. I am grateful for what they did for me, and I am aware that it was my life and my creative process.

Perhaps these examples illustrate how valuable it can be to know how to work with the yin and yang energies in a functional balance in your life.

*See Appendix Two for a list of **The Love Principles,** which can help you to keep focused on your power to open your heart center and change your life.*

10

Yin and Yang In a Balanced Life

We began our exploration with the questions, "How did this happen?" or, "How could I be so lucky?" or, "How can I change my life so that I feel more fulfilled?" I hope by now you have a grasp of how the interaction of the yin and yang forces brings things into being and how you can change your life through conscious direction of those polarities. When we are essentially unconscious of the interplay between yin and yang, we feel like we have no control over our lives. Good things feel almost like miracles, and we seem helpless to avert bad things.

Now that you have some understanding of these two polarities, you can create consciously the life you want to live.* You will want to bring the two forces into balance in your body, psyche and spirit. And you will be able to practice shifting back and forth between yin and yang expression in your relationships with others.

As Richard Lawrence expressed it: *Once you start to realize that all life is a balance between these two opposing, yet inseparable forces, you can improve any area of your life. The key is getting them to pull in the direction you want your life to take.***

It will be helpful if you can maintain a balance in your activities, within a day, a week, a month, and a year. You will not always be able to manage that, but you can make a concerted effort. Take stock of your daily schedule. Is there a good mix of relaxation, recreation and renewal (yin) to balance out your work (yang)? As you look at your weeks, is the pace of every day the same? If so, is it a balanced pace? If not, can you set aside your weekends for time alone, rest, and renewal (yin)?

If your days are reasonably balanced, it will be easier to create a balance in your weeks and years. If you hear yourself observing that you haven't had a day off in weeks, you will almost certainly be out of balance on the yang side and begin to experience stress and exhaustion.

However on all levels, physical, emotional, mental and spiritual, it is important to seek out polarizing influences – persons, ideas and experiences that are the opposite of what you ordinarily prefer, whether you find them in alternate world views, in differing traditions or cultures, in books, or in coworkers and companions. Polarities are life-giving.

Even opposition and antagonism can galvanize you to stand firm in your own convictions and to speak out for what you believe. If you settle into comfort zones of familiarity and do not challenge yourself with what is new and different, you will find that you move through your life in relative unconsciousness. A balance of yin and yang should not lead to a stability that is deadening. Rather, it should be life-giving and energizing, leading to new creative expressions of your inner potential.

It is important not to confuse styles of expression with the yin and yang forces themselves. Styles are expressions of different personality types. In our society, we tend to associate yang energy with hard-driving, aggressive men and yin energy with compliant and submissive women. However, in fact yang energy can be expressed gently and yin energy can be surprisingly tough.

It is not so much *how* you express the two forces that is important, but rather that you give full life to both of them. In yang energy you can be insistent without being harsh, you can initiate without being pushy, and you can encourage without being demanding. In yin energy you can receive without caving in, you can support without fawning, you can nurture without becoming codependent. You can choose the qualities that will characterize your expression of the two forces, qualities that are in harmony with your preferred style of interaction.

A balanced life should be dynamic, constantly shifting and changing. Your body gives you an illustration of dynamic balance every day. When you stand on both feet, you are balanced, but small muscles are constantly adjusting, tightening (yang) and relaxing (yin), in order to maintain the balance. Eventually even this balance becomes wearying and you feel the urge either to move, going more yang, or to relax by sitting down, which is more yin.

If you begin to walk, you express a different kind of balance. You shift your weight first to one side, then to the other. The balance is expressed in the motion.

The balanced expression of yin and yang in your life is like standing and walking. Sometimes there is more yin being expressed, sometimes more yang. Sometimes you are physically yang and yin in psyche and spirit. Sometimes the energies of spirit are heightened and activated (yang) and body and psyche go yin. And sometimes all the yang action is in feeling and thoughts while body and spirit are responsive and supportive in yin. The overall effect of such a life is balanced creativity.

If you live a balanced life in this fashion, you will be independent, self-reliant and creative while also being capable of intimacy and cooperation on all levels.

Perhaps what is most important is to make certain to take time to develop spiritually. As you do, you will be able to assume your role as a co-creator, not only in your own life, but in the world. The secret of co-creation is to express a balance of yin and yang energies in a dynamic and life-giving process. As you do so, you will be able to *create your own reality consciously rather than living as if you had no control over your life.****

See Appendix Two for a list of* **The Love Principles, *which can help you to keep focused on your power to open your heart center and change your life.*
***Page 36,* Little Book of Yin & Yang, *by Richard Lawrence, Great Britain: Thorsons, 2002.*
*** *This is one of* **The Love Principles** *[see Appendix Two].*

Postscript

A Tribute
To Arlene and Ed Kennedy

From the time I was very young, I sought union with God. As I came to know and understand the two polarities of that Creative Force, I discovered to my wonderment that I had been raised by two who were almost archetypal in their manifestation of the Great Yin and Yang.

On the occasion of their 50th wedding anniversary I wrote the following tribute to my parents. It seems a fitting postscript for this book.

Mother: a reflection of the feminine (yin) force. Ever a mystery to me as is the Great Mother — holding hidden in the innermost recesses of her heart the secrets of life — she freely taught me the outer forms of cooking, keeping house, caring for children, being a good friend, a faithful child, a responsible adult. But only by my own experience held in the shadow of her example could I learn the inner workings of her ease, flexibility, adaptability, dependability, endurance, loyalty, expansiveness and ability to nurture. She seemed always present, like a deeply rooted tree, strong and unbent by difficulties, moving through them with the ease of water finding a new course to run. She was constantly putting forth branches into new areas of interest that nourished her as the sun does a tree. Though calm and not easily upset, she nevertheless took on causes and served them with relentless dedication. Being of service in the world in her quiet and unassuming way was a powerful example for me. She didn't talk much about her convictions, but she expressed them in action. And when I expressed my opinions with loud conviction, she would respond with the quiet admonition: "What are you going to do about it?"

Mother seemed always to be there in my times of need. She would come and sit with me, bringing her steady presence as a healing balm. She didn't teach values with words, but rather by example. In all these ways she manifested the characteristic qualities of the Mother Force – that great and mysterious polarity of the God Force out of which all that is comes into being and on which we all feed and are sustained.

Father (Dad): a reflection of the masculine (yang) force. Energetic almost to a fault, he was constantly initiating activity, setting things in motion. Occasionally he came momentarily to rest, only to leap up again to be of service. He taught me to be independent, not only through his own example, but also through his encouragement. "You can do it" were his constantly nudging urges to activity followed by effusive praise at every small accomplishment. No matter if it was mechanical, social, educational, political, or financial in nature, he would offer a few key pointers for how to proceed and then gently nudge: "You can do it." I learned to be a fearless risk-taker, striking out boldly to do what I saw to do, felt needed doing, felt was right to do. Seldom did he offer criticism after the fact. Instead he would praise the effort and gently point out how to proceed on the next round.

His curious mind probed every corner of life experience, seeking to know and understand what made people the way they were, countries the way they are, life the way it is. Always the optimist, he would rebound quickly from even major set-backs and thrust forward with renewed energy in creating the new. Volatile, he would argue with me as we both flared in anger. And then he taught me forgiveness, for he never let me go to sleep without an exchange of reconciling love between us. Although his words of reprimand when I overstepped boundaries at home or at school reminded me of the values I had been taught, even more important was his example of unfaltering integrity as a businessman and community leader. In all these ways and more he manifested the yang polarity of the Creative Force that by its own initiating thrust causes activity to stir, and by its own ideas and models guides the purpose-driven expression of creativity.

These two became one, modeling for me the very inner union I longed for. The marriage they made is the union I sought of those two polarities within my own nature, They, in their outer expression, proved that it is possible to become one in the inner nature as well. They were like one being — whole, complete, coordinated in a harmonious rhythm of ease. The two had truly become one. Their union created an enormous, heart-center safe-space for me to grow in, to mature into my true nature. The home they built was a rock for me to stand on as I tried out my own life skills, and to return to when I needed to be replenished.

What greater gift could any child be given? A perfect environment in which to be nurtured and guided until I could blossom into my own uniqueness of being. It is for the blessing of that gift — the gift of their oneness in love — that I express my deep-felt gratitude to my parents, Arlene and Ed Kennedy.

Appendix One
Primary Characteristics of Yin and Yang

Yin

The primary characteristic of this force is that it gives form to the pattern which it has taken into its substance.

Receiving
 sustaining
 holding
 protecting
 yielding
 nurturing

Chaotic
 accommodating
 all-embracing

Yang

The primary characteristic of this force is that it sets the pattern for what will come into being.

Initiating
 catalyzing
 releasing
 risking
 resisting
 activating

Ordered
 discriminating
 selective

More on next page

accepting
both/and
breaks down
destructive

judging
either/or
builds up
constructive

Responding
offering options
detail-tending
permission-giving
reality-oriented
suggesting
forgiving
patient
diffuse

Directing
making choices
goal-setting
standard-setting
ideal-oriented
demanding
exacting
urgent
focused

Dark
obscuring
keeping hidden
mysterious
indirect

Light
revealing
making known
obvious / forthright
direct

Condensed
straight
hard
linear
unbending
inflexible
firm
closed
impenetrable
solid

Expanded
round
soft
circular
pliable
adaptable
yielding
open
permeable
hollow

Willful
passionate
active
determined

Expectant
dispassionate
attractive
allowing

Consistent
steady
transitory
evolving

Paradoxical
ever-changing
enduring
unfolding

More on next page

sequential
short-lived

Stimulating
arousing
evoking
energetic
impulsive
erratic
provoking

Penetrating
thrusting
pointed
pursuing
unrelenting
aggressive

cyclic
long-lasting

Calming
subduing
inhibiting
relaxed
dependable
regular
suppressing

Absorbing
holding
dull
inviting
rhythmic
passive

General Characteristics

cold	hot
wet	dry
light (weight)	heavy
dark	light
form	force
magnetic	electric
static	kinetic
effect	cause

More on next page

Common Associations

moon	sun
right-brain	left-brain
left side of body	right side of body
intuitive	logical
emotional	mental
existence	essence
material	spiritual
unconscious	conscious
winter	summer
creation	emanation
body	soul / psyche
body & soul	spirit
values communication, connection, community	values autonomy, individuality, self-sufficiency

Appendix Two

The Love Principles

The Love Principles were received by Arleen Lorrance in 1970 while she was teaching in a ghetto high school in Brooklyn, New York. Two books written by Arleen Lorrance tell the story of the first Love Project in Brooklyn (*The Love Project*, LP Publications, 1972) and how the principles can help to transform your life (*The Love Principles*, Teleos Imprint Wisdom Books, 2001). The books are available on amazon.com and on our website: www.teleosinstitute.com.

The six **Love Principles** have been the basis for the work Arleen Lorrance and the author have done together for 40 years. It is our purpose to enhance the development of the spiritual consciousness of individuals. We intend to take individuals beyond the material to an integration of sensing, feeling, thinking and intuition so that they can function as whole, conscious beings who embody heart-centered, unconditional love. *The Love Principles* are key to this process.

Please see the next page for a list of the six principles.

The Love Principles
as received by Arleen Lorrance in 1970:

✦ *Receive all persons as beautiful exactly as they are (including self).*

✦ *Be the change you want to see, instead of trying to change anyone else.*

✦ *Create your own reality consciously, rather than living as if you have no control over your life.*

✦ *Provide others with opportunities to give.*

✦ *Have no expectations, but rather abundant expectancy.*

✦ *Problems are opportunities.*

The six principles function as one sentence, linked together by the recognition that *Choice is the life process.* In every new moment of awareness, you are free to make a new choice.

CPSIA information can be obtained
at www.ICGtesting.com
Printed in the USA
LVHW092110051221
705373LV00004B/83